A Journey

In The

Wilderness

Becoming Fruitful In The Kingdom

By

Paul K. Weigel

Published By:
Mass Communications Inc.

E-mail: ajourney@theforerunner.net

Website: http://www.theforerunner.net

Distributed In Canada By
Rainbow House
1-800-265-8887

ISBN 1-895960-10-X

A Journey In The Wilderness -
Becoming Fruitful In The Kingdom

Published by: Mass Communications Inc.
E-mail: ajourney@theforerunner.net
Website: http://www.theforerunner.net

All Scripture quotations are from the Authorized Version of the Bible unless notated.

Cover design and layout by: Mass Communications Inc.
Cover photographs by: Paul K. Weigel

The Online Bible program was used to assemble this book.
Thanks to Larry Pierce and David Pohl.
Copies of the program can be had at:
http://www.OnlineBible.org

Canadian Cataloguing in Publication Data

Weigel, Paul K. (Paul Kenneth), 1950-
A journey in the wilderness : becoming fruitful in the kingdom

ISBN: 1-895960-10-X

1. Christian life. 2. Church work. I. Title

BV4501.2W4163 2000 248.4 C00-930770-2

Printed in Canada

Dedication

*To my precious Melissa,
to whom, I pray, that these
truths will guide into your
special place of Kingdom fruitfulness.*

Table of Contents

Acknowledgements

Much of the content of this book came to me as a series of revelations during the years from 1986 to 1989. These revelations were a response to a "calling out" for understanding as to what God was doing in my life. I had sold a successful business to follow Him in what I believed to be a call to ministry. God had other plans. He wanted to prepare me for ministry first. I never dreamt that it would take almost 13 years and that He would use those outward foolish looking experiences and these revelations to be a part of my ministry to the Body of Christ.

One of the great mercies of God to me was that He gave me a prayer partner through some of this journey. His persistence and continual seeking of the Lord for "the next step" was one of the reasons I didn't give up on scores of occasions. There were countless days spent seeking the Lord together, trying to find a place of understanding. Many times we thought we were crazy for the risks we were taking with our lives. Either we were right in what we were hearing, or we were going to be complete fools. I am thankful to the Lord for David Hall, and for his contribution to my journey in the Wilderness.

There were others too many to name who, for a season, prayed or played some other role appointed by the Lord in my process of sanctification. They were knowingly or unknowing serving me and the Lord with their gift of grace.

Special thanks to Jeanette Duncan, Margaret Kennedy, and Ken Waite for their work editing the manuscript.

Introduction

The Heart of every Christian who loves his Lord and Saviour is to serve and please Him. Scripture describes us as vessels of silver and gold that must first be prepared or sanctified in order to be of honor. Although God's love for us is unconditional, we desire, because of love, that His purpose for our lives be fulfilled unto honour and unto glory to Him. God's preparation is not a PhD in theology, but a consuming fire which purges the dross of our Hearts, so we can do God's work, God's way, from a pure Heart. This is vital to achieving our "call" in the way in which **He** will get the glory. Although the redeeming work of God is a lifelong process, there is a distinct season of God's purging which follows a definable, systematic pattern for the Church and every Spirit-filled Christian. Worldwide, the Body of Christ is entering this season of purging. We are being called into the Wilderness in preparation for the most difficult and glorious time in the history of the Church. We are being prepared as the Church who will overcome the Devil, the Flesh, and the world. We are being prepared to rule and reign with Jesus in this Age and in the Age to Come. We are being readied as the Bride of Christ for the Marriage Feast of the Lamb. We are being prepared for our ministry to God.

God has revealed to us in Scripture a pattern of the process of sanctification and instruction outlining how we must respond to His work so we do not fight against it and become derelict in the Wilderness. Many Christians who are in the Wilderness misinterpret the purpose and objectives of the circumstance and rebel against God's purging work without discerning what He is doing. Some Christians won't enter the Wilderness because they don't or won't believe that God is anything but their carnal definition of "good". We can either cooperate with His preparation or knowingly or unknowingly resist it. Scripture reveals God's ways of working which can only be seen when looking at the overview of circumstance. These patterns in the Christian life are designed to give us the "big picture" view of our day-to-day lives in light of God's objectives and perspective. How we respond to God's preparation will determine whether we will become vessels unto honour or vessels unto dishonour.

When we sacrifice our lives on the altar of refining fire, we prove that God is truly Lord of our life and that we love Him and trust His sanctifying work. Our trust and surrender is as much glorifying to God as any thing we could do for Him, **because God looks on the Heart.**

But in a great house there are not only vessels of gold and of silver, but also of wood and of earth; and some to honour, and some to dishonour. ***If a man therefore purge himself from these, he shall be a vessel unto honour, sanctified,*** *and meet for the master's use, [and] prepared unto every good work. Flee also youthful lusts: but follow righteousness, faith, charity, peace, with them that call on the Lord out of a* ***pure heart****. 2 Timothy 2: 20.*

No discipline seems pleasant at the time, but painful. Later on, however, it produces a harvest of righteousness and peace for those who have been trained by it. Therefore, strengthen your feeble arms and weak knees. "Make level paths for your feet," ***so that the lame may not be disabled, but rather healed.*** *Make every effort to live in peace with all men and to be holy; without holiness no one will see the Lord. Hebrews 12:11-14.* NIV

Every man's work shall be made manifest: for the day shall declare it, because it shall be revealed by fire; ***and the fire shall try every man's work of what sort it is****. If any man's work abide which he hath built thereupon, he shall receive a reward. If any man's work shall be burned, he shall suffer loss: but he himself shall be saved; yet so as by fire. 1 Cor. 3:13-15.*

Chapter One

Becoming Fruitful In The Kingdom

Therefore say I unto you, the kingdom of God shall be taken from you, and given to a nation bringing forth the fruits thereof. And whosoever shall fall on this stone shall be broken: but on whomsoever it shall fall, it will grind him to powder. Matt. 21:42-43

The Scriptures document many instances of God's discipline, purging and sanctifying process in preparation for ministry. They are examples for us of how God calls us and then prepares us before we are commissioned into service. In the most recent years, there have been many prophetic words proclaiming that God is raising up an army. This is the "call". The process of sanctification is the "boot camp" of preparation which precedes it.

Part of our makeup as human beings is to find a purpose for our life. God made us this way so He could fulfill us with **His** purpose and thereby bring pleasure to us, and glory to Him. It is part of His plan for His Body. As a member of the Body of Christ, every person has a unique place of service. We were reborn into this new life which is characterized by abundant fruitfulness, to bear fruit. It is not our efforts which produce fruitfulness but rather, fruitfulness is the work of the Holy Spirit. Our calling to service to Jesus is not necessarily some physical activity (although it often is), rather, it is a spiritual cooperation with the Holy Spirit to produce fruitfulness not only in others' lives, but first and foremost in our own lives.

Our North American concept of fruitfulness is not necessarily God's concept of fruitfulness. We may have visions of preaching to a football stadium of people or praying for the sick. We may have thoughts of successful ministry through business and giving millions of dollars to the work of the Kingdom. All of these things may be a result of fruitfulness. This, however, is not the essence of fruitfulness, but rather the manifestation of it. Fruitfulness is the acquisition of the treasure of the Kingdom. Receiving life from the Holy Spirit and surrendering to His pruning will produce the fruit of the Kingdom of God which is our first service to Him. Therefore, this process of sanctification is for every Believer. Every person who confesses Christ as Lord and Saviour is destined for sanctification, purging, and preparation to reign forever with Him. We are commanded to be fruitful by abiding in the ongoing flow of life and sanctification of Jesus (Matt. 15:1-8). It is His work in us which produces the fruit, and it is the fruit which is our ministry to God. Outward signs of ministry may not necessarily be fruitfulness since Jesus warned about doing the work of the Kingdom out of an impure motive. These can be dead works which do not flow out of the life we draw from Christ.

"But seek first his kingdom and his righteousness, and all these things will be given to you as well." Matt 6:33 NIV articulates this view of our service to God: to become what He has called us to seek to be and the rest of life will fall into place. It sets our surrender to the discipline, purification and the sanctification process as the highest priority in any Believer's life. Our surrender and cooperation with this purpose is our first ministry to God. It is through our becoming like Him that we overcome the Flesh, the world, and the Devil. This brings glory to God.

The Process Of Sanctification

On one particular day, at one particular time, you and I each entered into the Kingdom of God. We were outside looking in. Then in a moment, we were translated from death into eternal life. As marvellous and wonderful as that was, it was only the beginning of our salvation. Since that time, the Holy Spirit has revealed righteousness to us. He has led us to repent, denounce, and confess our sin, thereby bringing us into the abundant life. Jesus came to us to lead us into eternal and abundant life. Scripture doesn't always delineate about which it speaks, but we know that we are saved (eternal life) and are being saved (abundant life). In one sense, everything was done for us in that moment in time when we entered eternal life; in another sense, we are just at the beginning of acquiring the abundant life. We are sanctified, and in the process of being sanctified. Therefore, for our purposes, the "Process" of sanctification will always refer to our acquisition of the abundant life.

Scripture clearly defines for us the road to eternal life and it clearly defines the path to abundant life. The Process of God's sanctification is more obscure in Scripture than the steps to eternal life, but, nevertheless, He has made it evident for those who diligently seek to find it. The Process is defined, systematic, and identifiable as is the path to eternal life.

He has revealed His process of sanctification in Scripture so that we would understand His process and cooperate with it. For some who have not come to this understanding, it will give meaning to the past. For others, it will be revelation as to how they have been resisting the Holy Spirit's work out of ignorance or misunderstanding. Ultimately, a fresh and clear understanding of God's process of sanctification will bring a new sense of destiny, vision and calling which we need in order to continue saying "yes" to the Holy Spirit's work. If we can see ourselves in the process of death to self and believe in faith that God will raise up a new man, alive in Christ, then in that instance, we have overcome the Flesh, the world, and the Devil and have acquired more of the abundant life.

God does not leave us in the pain we are in. He has created us for pleasure and wants to restore us to that purpose. Complete redemption restores us to His original purpose.

His purging of our sin and past pain is one of the greatest acts of love in the history of the universe. With one word, He created the Heavens and the earth, but it took the blood of His Son to rescue us from the fear, stubbornness, and rebellion inherent in the Adamic Nature. There is a hostility, the Scriptures say, between the Adamic Nature of man and the Holy Spirit. God's Process is putting that hostility of the Adamic Nature to death, step by step, so that we are no longer at enmity with God. Some Believers are afraid to admit that there are still unredeemed areas in their lives where the Adamic Nature is alive and is in fact, hostile to God. They feel that if God knew about their rebellion and anger toward Him, He would be angry. They suppress these thoughts rather than expose these areas for God to redeem. Nothing is hidden from God, and it is His way to expose these things so that we may take our hostility toward Him, to the cross. We need not fear God because every Believer is being redeemed from their enmity toward Him. The purpose of the Process is to fully redeem us to Christ, and in that, there is intimacy with the Father and abundant life. As you can well imagine, the unredeemed areas of the Adamic Nature are "the little foxes that spoil the vine" of intimacy with Christ (Song of Solomon 2:15). The depth of intimacy with God is determined by the level of death to the Adamic Nature that the Believer has experienced. No amount of striving will build our dependence, trust, and love for God. Only walking with Him in the valley of the shadow of death and having Him deliver us into new life will lay the foundation for intimacy with Him.

...If any man will come after me, let him deny himself, and take up his cross, and follow me. For whosoever will save his life shall lose it: and whosoever will lose his life for my sake shall find it. Matt. 16:24-25

The perfect life for Christians is walking in obedience to the Holy Spirit because it is in walking obedient to the Holy Spirit that we will completely fulfill the purposes of God, and not the lusts of the Flesh. It is not for want of trying that we fail to walk in the Spirit. It is that we have an enemy of the Spirit, which is alive in us, which is the Adamic Nature. Although the process of sanctification is ongoing throughout the Believer's entire life, there are distinct seasons of purging which produce an ever increasing ability to walk in the Spirit of God. The greater the obedience we have to the Holy Spirit, the greater the ministry we have to God. It is this obedience that only He can see, that produces intimacy with God, joy, and peace. This is the abundant life, and the foundation for fulfilling our call.

As unpleasant as it may be, it is in life's valleys that we find our Saviour.

There He is, confident and sure,
unmoved by the darkness that frightens me.
I take His hand and when I do, I know He is completely in control,
and that my fear is totally unwarranted,
even an affront to His love for me.
I hang my head in my failing;
unable to trust the love that saved me before, and will save me now.
He gently lifts my head and smiles,
and in that instant, I am delivered of my fear,
for I have seen and experienced again, the love of my Father.

It is humbling to see ourselves in light of the perfect love of Jesus. It is that humbling of the Heart which acquires grace and grace is the currency of Heaven. It is through grace we were saved and are being saved. It is humbling that entitles us to grace because: "God gives grace to the humble" (James 4:6). The Flesh (Adamic Nature) vehemently opposes humbling, yet there is no other way to be saved. Our choice in the battle between Flesh and Spirit wins the war. Our choice can bring the power of the blood of Jesus to our aid or grieve the Spirit away. Our right to choose is man's greatest power because it will determine our destiny. We either put the Flesh to death through the power of the Spirit, or strengthen the power of the Flesh in our lives by our choice. The Adamic Nature attempts to deceive us into making the Flesh lord. The benefits are short term, and we soon see, that we have traded our birthright for a bowl of stew.

The Holy Spirit will always lead us into death of the Flesh. Sometimes that death is in the form of suffering and humility. It is His job to create just the right circumstances to drive a stake through the "Heart" of the Flesh. When He does, He resurrects with Christ the New Man in the Spirit. The things Jesus suffered taught Him obedience to the Spirit. He perfectly fulfilled His ministry to His Father and man because He walked in obedience to the Spirit.

This is what it means to take up our cross and follow Him. It is to choose death, suffering and humility, in order to be reborn of the Spirit, and to live the abundant life. The cost is high, but the rewards make it a bargain.

...that he (Jesus) might sanctify and cleanse it (the Church) with the washing of water by the word, that he might present it to himself a glorious church, not having spot, or wrinkle, or any such thing; but that it should be holy and without blemish. Eph. 5:26-27

Jesus is preparing us and the Church, not for ministry as we would think of it, but for the Marriage Feast, (Matt. 22:4) where we will take our role as His Bride and rule and reign with Him for all eternity. As with any Bride before the wedding, she is preparing for the biggest day of her life.

Everything must be perfect with no detail too small to which to attend. And so it is with the Church in these days, just before the return of our Bridegroom. Jesus is preparing us for the biggest day in the history of the universe. He will not return to find His Bride in disarray. She will be perfect, glorious, wonderful, and wholly in love with Her Bridegroom. When Jesus was tempted in the Wilderness, He was victorious because the Devil "found nothing in Him". He was wholly the Father's and wholly directed and controlled by the Holy Spirit. Will we, as the Church, ever be wholly directed and controlled by the Holy Spirit? Fortunately for us, the role of the Holy Spirit is to sanctify us and prepare us. Our part in the process is to say "yes" to the Spirit's work.

Jesus was baptised in the Holy Spirit. Then, immediately after this, the Holy Spirit "drove" Him into the Wilderness to be tested. After He came out of the Wilderness, He began His public ministry. This is a paradigm which says something of the time clock marking Jesus' return. In 1906, the Azusa Street revival marked the beginning of the greatest outpouring of the Holy Spirit to the common man that has been seen since the birth of the Church. The book of Joel talks of the early and latter rain, and the early and latter outpouring of the Holy Spirit. The Scriptures reveal the outpouring of the Holy Spirit in the early Church. Most recently, there has been the "Latter Rain" outpouring of the Holy Spirit from 1906 through to about 1980. That season being over, the Church is in a season of preparation or testing prior to it being unveiled as the glorious Bride of Christ. Having been baptised in the Holy Spirit, the Church is now being driven into the Wilderness for a time of purging and testing.

God's order in dealing with His people is: first, His prophets, then secondly His leaders, thirdly, the general Body of Christ, and then finally, He will judge the world. This season of refining has not gone unnoticed by many of God's prophets. Ten years ago, no one was interested in talking about God's process of sanctification, but now there are prophetic teachings and songs being written about it. God is calling His people into the "Wilderness" for a time of preparation for His return. Most of the Children of Israel died in the Wilderness because they rebelled against His refining process. So also will our power of choice determine our destiny. Psalms 103:7 says: "*He made known his ways unto Moses, his acts unto the children of Israel*". We are a nation of kings and priests, filled with the Holy Spirit. God intends to make known His ways to us, as a Church, that we may not sin against Him in this Process. He wants to reveal His ways of refining so we will cooperate with Him. Making wise choices will result in our being fully prepared in what will be the Church's most glorious hour, just before Jesus, our Lover, returns for us.

Chapter Two

Preparation For Our Ministry

With every Christian, God does His preparation in a different way and in a different time. Illustrations of people's lives documented in Scripture indicate that His objectives are the same, but His methods vary with each individual. He creates circumstances which teach, humble, and bring self discovery. He is a master sanctifier who takes us to our limit, but never over it. He pushes our "buttons" and exposes our Heart. He shows us our motives and still loves us enough to bless us in spite of our fallen nature.

God's purposes in preparation are to bring purity, wisdom, and perseverance. These things can't be learned from books or sermons. These may help to bring understanding, but character can only be developed through experience.

Any parent knows that it is very difficult to let your child make a mistake. Yet without learning the lessons discovered in failing, the child cannot mature. Our failures and our sufferings can teach us and make us obedient, or can make us hardened. When we respond the wrong way, as the Children of Israel did in the Wilderness, it only prolongs the Process. God's persistent discipline may seem severe at the time, but when we are trained by Him and enter into the peaceful fruit of righteousness, we discover that His purging work is a demonstration of His mercy and kindness to us.

If you are not disciplined (and everyone undergoes discipline), then you are illegitimate children and not true sons. Moreover, we have all had human fathers who disciplined us and we respected them for it. How much more should we submit to the Father of our spirits and live! Our fathers disciplined us for a little while as they thought best; but God disciplines us for our good, that we may share in his holiness. No discipline seems pleasant at the time, but painful. Later on, however, it produces a harvest of righteousness and peace for those who have been trained by it. Heb. 12:8-11 NIV

All of the great men of the Bible were prepared for their ministry by God. These men were quite ordinary before God did His work of preparation. Most of them had obvious character flaws which God healed and strengthened so that their weakness became their greatest strength. When we worship Jesus and the Father in Heaven for all eternity, it will be in part because of His masterful redemption of His beloved Bride. We will overcome enemies much stronger than ourselves because of His "fathering" in our life. We think that when we meet Moses or King David or the Apostle Paul in Heaven, we will be in awe of their exploits, but we have the same God as they do, and He has not changed. They were just as broken and weak as we are, yet God caused them to conquer their enemies. This is one of the most important messages of the Bible. God can do powerful things with anyone who is surrendered to Him. In this season of restoration and glorification of the Church, we can expect that God will sanctify his prophets, teachers, apostles, evangelists and pastors. He will strengthen them so that the Devil will have nothing in which to gain a foothold in their life. He will armor them with righteousness and cause them to overcome the Flesh, the world, and the Devil. Scripture chronicles some of the patriarchs' journey with God. Those journeys reveal some of the ways God prepares His people for their ministry. Their lives have become examples for our own personal preparation for ministry.

Moses

Moses was an important figure in the history of God's people. He demonstrated one aspect of Jesus' role to us as deliverer. God's preparation for Moses' ministry started before he was born. God not only preserved Moses' life, but also provided for his education when he was adopted into Pharaoh's household. His early identification with his people and the killing of the abusive Egyptian may be indications of both his weakness and his motivation, and also his hatred for injustice. Nonetheless, this action drove him into the Wilderness where he spent the next 40 years tending sheep. This was the preparation of Moses for his ministry of leadership, intercession, and prophecy to Egypt and to the Children of Israel. He learned about the Wilderness and about managing sheep. He was also humbled a great deal from his former life in the courts of the Pharaoh. Most certainly there were times when he wondered if his choice to leave Pharaoh's court and become like his people was the right one. In the natural, it seemed like the all-time blunder of blunders. He was in exile from Egypt and his people. He could have assumed a role of authority in the Egyptian government. In man's eyes, he had failed. Moses had to accept, even if he failed, that he had done what he believed was right. This was an important part of his preparation because he was later described as the humblest man on the face of the earth at the time. He wasn't born humble. He was humbled by the circumstances he lived through.

The term "humble" is often misunderstood. Humility can be defined as a view of ourselves in light of who God is. Moses discovered God while in the midst of his humble circumstances. The Wilderness taught Moses dependency on God, which was necessary for the deliverance of the Children of Israel. His work with the sheep was not unlike his leadership role of Israel. His education was important because he needed to speak to Pharaoh, not as an uneducated slave, but as a former member of his court. It was also important for him in his leadership of Israel to have a formal education.

In the early stages of Moses' role as deliverer of Israel, he seemed afraid of what he had himself into. As he saw the power of God come to deliver Israel and confirm his leadership, he became more confident. During his 40 years in the Wilderness, Moses developed a relationship with God which was the foundation for his preparation for ministry. It was his revelation of God that produced his humility, then his vision, then his dedication, and finally his authority. Because He had grown to know and trust God, he was able to lead two million people out of Egypt into a land they did not know. Moses knew He could not do it in his own power and that He would have to depend on God to do it. It was this dependence on God that made him prepared and ready. The very fact that he felt unable to do it was an indication that he was ready to allow God to do it through Him. When Moses killed the Egyptian soldier, he was not surrendered to God. He was doing what He thought was God's work, in his own way. It was the work of his Flesh, not the Spirit of God. Much of the Church's ministry today is good things done in human ways. This does not please God neither does it accomplish His purposes. After forty years in the Wilderness, under God's sanctifying process, Moses emerged as a man fully surrendered and trusting in God. Only then could God use him to do powerful exploits through which His purposes were accomplished. Moses allowed God to be revealed through him to Israel, the Egyptians, and all the nations around them.

David

King David's preparation was different, but in some ways similar to that of Moses. As a young man, he spent time learning to shepherd sheep and to build his relationship with the Lord. Early in his life, his gift of faith began to be demonstrated in fearless acts of courage to defend his sheep. As a young boy, he killed a lion and a bear with few or no weapons. By the time he came to be an armor bearer for Saul, he was familiar with how the Spirit of God had been working through him. He had a gift of faith for the moment and the personal faith of experience to support his "call". He was also being prepared by serving in the court of the King of Israel, particularly in the area of war and battle. He learned some of the basic principles of ruling a nation and he learned some things which a leader should not do. God often prepares us by showing us what not to do. Soon after his defeat of the Philistine army, David found himself graduating from his practical education as a "ruler in training" to his development as a man of godly character. He was falsely accused by Saul and had to escape to avoid being killed. He was innocent but driven into the Wilderness by circumstances beyond his control. It was in the Wilderness God humbled him and tested him. Twice, David had an opportunity to slay Saul and both times he refused to take his "call" to be king into his own hands. David was made king by an act of God. Although David was a mighty warrior, he understood that he could not make a place for himself. He waited for God to raise him up. As long as Saul was alive, he understood it was not time for him to be King. He knew that if he were to rule in the power of the Holy Spirit, he could not take control of his life, but would have to surrender to the timing and way God wanted to make him King. David did not seek power or authority, but was given them as he surrendered to the Holy Spirit. David demonstrated the same type of surrender that Christ had for His Father. This is what it means to give up your life, to gain it. (Matt. 16:25)

It was God who had David in the Wilderness, and who would bring him back when He had achieved His goal of preparing him for his ministry to Israel. Even when Saul finally died, he waited for another 16 months before taking his position as King of Judah. His life was not his own. He was completely surrendered to the Holy Spirit. There was in David no love of position or lust for power. His love was for God. The Psalms that David wrote reveal a deep love and trust for God. This love and surrender was developed, in part, in the things he suffered in the Wilderness. He was filled with the same Holy Spirit we are. He did not receive these character traits by some special act of God. He was prepared by God for his ministry. He was called to rule over a nation. We are called to rule over the things of this world in the Holy Spirit. David became a great leader and man of God not in a day or a week or a few months. David learned to surrender to the Holy Spirit and show humility toward God so that He could become what God "called" him to be. He did not get the love, trust, surrender, and humility that was the foundation for his service to God in some supernatural event, but over years of preparation by Saul's side and in the Wilderness. Somewhere in this preparation, David came to see that his relationship with God was the center of life. Anything else that life could offer was of no real value except in obedience to God. When he danced naked before the Lord, it was an expression of his total disregard for the values of this world, and his supreme regard for his relationship with God as the central focus and reason for living. He was not trapped in the temporal, trivial pursuit of being a King. He was first, a lover of God. David was an example for us of a man who was fully human, with victories and failings, being prepared, used, and pleasing to God.

Joseph

Joseph was called by God to become a type of saviour for his people. This would bring glory to God. What He was able to do through Joseph was recorded for our benefit. It proves that God is able to provide for his people, and has a plan for that provision many years in advance. It also reveals how God prepares ordinary people so that His power and provision will flow through them.

Joseph's story was designed by God to reveal Himself and His ways. Joseph was the favourite son of his father. Joseph was unwise and cocky in his attitude toward his brothers. He inflamed their jealousy by flaunting the dream of his older brothers serving him. Why did God give the dream? He knew the potential risk for a reaction between Joseph and his brothers. It was part of His plan. It was the prophetic dream that drove Joseph into his personal Wilderness and forward into the fulfilment of his calling and the purpose of God. In the midst of his rejection and life-threatening circumstances, God was fully in control and working out His plan.

Joseph was bought by Potifer, an officer of Pharaoh. His gifting, as a prophet and as an administrator, was given an opportunity to be used within the household. He spent some time there learning the practical skills of administrating. When he had accomplished this portion of his preparation, he was propositioned by Potifer's wife. Joseph responded to the situation, not out of his need, but out of his relationship with God and loyalty for his master. These were the two things that would be necessary for his successful ministry as an administrator second-in-command to Pharaoh. Loyalty and self control were prerequisites. Had he not passed this test, he would have had to go back and relearn the lesson. The test itself became the agent to move him along to the next stage of his preparation. He was falsely accused and imprisoned. It was in prison that Joseph's prophetic gifting was developed. He also further developed his administrative gift. God chose prison as the venue for that preparation because it was a humbling place. If Joseph became a powerful man and provided for the Egyptians, but refused his brothers when they came for food, then God's plan would have failed. Joseph's Heart had to be softened and filled with compassion. Compassion comes from the experience of pain. While in prison, Joseph thought about his home and his family. He longed for them and desired to be in fellowship with them. It was the longing for his family that brought him to forgiveness and healing. There was further preparation as well. When Joseph interpreted the first dream, he said (to paraphrase), "*Please remember me, here in prison, and get me out.*" He was struggling to get himself released from prison. God, however, did not release him at this time. Two more years passed before he was released through no effort of his own. What happened, during those two years in prison that was so necessary for his full preparation? Scripture does not reveal specifically what happened, but if we place ourselves in the same circumstances, we may see how that time in prison tested Joseph's faith. He surely remembered the dream and wondered if it would ever be fulfilled. He thought about all the injustice he had suffered. He probably questioned why God had him in these circumstances and how He was able to deliver him, but didn't. These difficult tests of his faith were the grains of sand that made his pearl of great price.

Moreover he called for a famine upon the land: he brake the whole staff of bread. He sent a man before them, even Joseph, who was sold for a servant whose feet they hurt with fetters. He was laid in iron until the time that his word came. ***The word of the LORD tried him***. Psalms 105:16-19 NIV

Somewhere during those two additional years in prison, Joseph accepted God's authority in his life. He stopped struggling to get out of jail and embraced all God had for him where He was. He came to accept that even if he spent the rest of his life in prison he had all he needed to be happy and fulfilled - God. He also came to realize that it was God's mercy and love for him that had him where he was. When he emerged from prison, he was a compassionate, humble, wise, and faithful man. He was fully prepared in the use of his gifting and in character, which were critical to the success of his calling. Without this preparation, he probably would have sent his brothers away without his help. Joseph acted as God acts toward us - with love and compassion even though he was rejected and treated unjustly. Joseph remained faithful to God even in suffering and rejection and He was made by God more like Himself. When he finally became the second most powerful man in Egypt, he was able to handle that power without it destroying his character and values. If God had given Joseph the prophetic power and prosperity when he was a young man, he would have misused it. He may have flaunted it and "lorded" it over people, instead of humbly using it for the good of others. He may have used his own understanding instead of depending on God for wisdom. Many people when given power have been destroyed by it, or have brutalized others with it. The qualities of our Hearts and our surrender to the sanctifying work of the Holy Spirit makes the gifts of God fruitful in the Kingdom. Without God's preparation, we would be unable to handle the power and authority He wants to give us. At any point in Joseph's preparation, he could have failed to cooperate with God. He could have refused to forgive, or succumbed to Potifer's wife as a way of comforting himself in his alienation from his home and family, but he didn't. He put his faith in God as his provider and deliverer, even in the time of testing.

The true measure of our maturity as Believer's is not how much we know, or how well we serve. It is measured by the degree of difficult circumstances and suffering we can overcome through our faith in God. The more difficult the circumstances, the closer we are to the fulfilment or release of our true call.

Paul

It was by God's design that Paul was born in Tarsus. In the early stages of Paul's life, this fact may have seemed insignificant, but later it became an integral part of God's plan for Paul's life and call. It proves that God has every detail of His plan for a Believer's life carefully worked out right from the beginning. Paul was educated in Jerusalem with the most influential theologians of the day. He was a Pharisee and quite zealous by nature. He persecuted the Church as part of his misguided service to God. When he was knocked off his horse on the road to Damascus and converted, he was immediately humbled. He considered himself to be pious and a defender of the laws of God. In his conversion, he realized that in spite of all his learning, he had not found God. He was blinded, and it was necessary for him to be lead around by others. He was faced with the prospect of being blind for the rest of his life. The Church that he had persecuted, prayed for his healing. God rubbed Paul's nose in his own folly but it was good for him. He was already being de-programmed from the way he used to think about God and His Kingdom and began to learn God's ways. Paul spent the next years of his life in his personal wilderness in Arabia. He earned a living as a tentmaker. As a Pharisee, a scholar and religious zealot, this was an occupation well below his stature. In Arabia, however, he needed to find a way to make a living and as humbling as it was, tent making was it.

When Paul began his teaching ministry, he was able to communicate the truths about the Gospel with a perspective on the Old Covenant. He drew valuable comparisons between the old and the new covenants for the Church. His preaching was so powerful that he was threatening to the Jews and the gentiles. He had persecuted the Church, and persecution was now his main opposition. Persecution is the fuel which feeds the fire of passion and purity. Paul required great dedication and commitment to conquer the opposition and difficulties that faced him. He was a man characterized by zeal and single mindedness. He was focused on completing the call, at all costs. He was the right man for the call, with the right gift, who was **fully** prepared by God.

Ordinary Men

The Scriptures recount the lives of ordinary men whom God used to bring a witness of Himself and to demonstrate His love for all people. The preparation for the call was critical to their success. In the lives of the godly men of the Bible, God used adversity, rejection, and difficulty of all manner to shape and mould their character. It was these difficulties which prepared and humbled them to minister. The trials shaped who they became, and who they became was their preparation for fruitful ministry.

There are three stages to the preparation: formal education and knowledge, the development and use of the Believer's gifts, and the humbling and development of the person's Heart. Proverbs 24:3-4 says that a house is built on three things; wisdom, understanding and knowledge.

God has revealed in many Scriptures that every detail of our preparation has been planned. He has also revealed His methods of preparation. Not even Jesus escaped the testing of the Wilderness. God's preparation of our lives is perfect. The parents to whom we were born, the town in which we grew up, and the friends we have had, good or bad, all have contributed to our preparation, to fulfill the purpose for which we were created. If we feel that we could have done more, or had a better chance to be what God wants for our life, "if only......", then we are accusing God of making a mistake with us. Only He knows how He will fulfill the call He placed on our life before we were born. We have a destiny which was established when God created Adam. He knew us then and appointed this time and in this way to fulfill His purpose for our life. All we can do to mess that up is to exercise our right of choice and go our own way. The Children of Israel rebelled and refused to trust God with their lives. They accused Him of not really loving and caring for them. They could not move forward in God because they did not believe He would make all their difficulties into the fulfilment of His promise to them. They didn't understand that they had to be prepared to enter the Promise of God. Even Paul warned us about the war that rages in us to lead us to spend our lives in pursuit of comfort and fleshly desires.

Those who live according to the sinful nature, have their minds set on what that nature desires; but those who live in accordance with the Spirit, have their minds set on what the Spirit desires. The mind of sinful man is death, but the mind controlled by the Spirit is life and peace; the sinful mind is hostile to God. It does not submit to God's law, nor can it do so. Those controlled by the sinful nature, cannot please God. Romans 8: 5-8 NIV

The Adamic Nature is hostile to God and His purposes for our life. We must be at war with the Flesh, so we don't become as the Children of Israel did and die, never knowing the fulfilment of completing the call God has appointed for us. Our serving the Flesh is subtle and easily justified by the rationale of the human nature. Only God can judge the motives and intentions of the Heart. He will judge our Hearts if we ask Him. He will fulfill us with more of Himself, and give more pleasure in Him than we thought possible. This is His promise to us:

"Although you have been forsaken and hated, with no-one travelling through, I will make you the everlasting pride and the joy of all generations. You will drink the milk of nations and be nursed at royal breasts. Then you will know that I, the LORD, am your Saviour, your Redeemer, the Mighty One of Jacob. Instead of bronze I will bring you gold, and silver in place of iron. Instead of wood I will bring you bronze, and iron in place of stones. I will make peace your governor and righteousness your ruler. No longer will violence be heard in your land, nor ruin or destruction within your borders, but you will call your walls Salvation and your gates Praise. The sun will no more be your light by day, nor will the brightness of the moon shine on you, for the LORD will be your everlasting light, and your God will be your glory. Your sun will never set again, and your moon will wane no more; the LORD will be your everlasting light, and your days of sorrow will end. Isa. 60:15-20 NIV

Chapter Three

The War Within

Scripture and preachers often refer to the Adamic Nature as the Fallen or Sin Nature, the Old Man, and the Flesh. The Sin Nature that we are born into has some specific characteristics which the Lord must redeem before He can make us an effective servant in His Kingdom. Similar to the concept of being saved and continuing to be saved, we have been saved from the Sin Nature and we are being saved from that Nature. The characteristics of this Nature are important for us to recognize so that we can more easily discern what is Spirit and what is Flesh. Our Heart is very deceptive and we can be deceived by the Flesh's trickery. The Spirit of God and the Flesh of man are at enmity with one another. They cannot cohabit. One will prevail over the other in every area of our life.

Water baptism symbolizes the death of the Old Man and the resurrection of the Spirit Man. It symbolizes what has been done, and what will be done in our life. We become the Spirit Man at conversion and the Old Man is sentenced to death. We are born again. This transformation is provided for us in full at our conversion, but it is being continuously accomplished by the sanctifying work of the Holy Spirit. The execution of the Old Man is a process. In the early stages of our walk with the Holy Spirit, the Adamic Nature has control of many areas of our life. As we walk with the Spirit in obedience, He redeems those areas and He takes control of them. This is the process of being set aside as wholly for the Lord. It is a life long process, but there is an intense season of purging which follows baptism in the Holy Spirit and which continues on, if surrendered to, until there is a revealing and unfolding of our purpose or call in God. The purpose or call may be something other than what is normally thought of as ministry, but it is always birthed and initiated by God. We do not choose it. He has chosen us and has called us to His heavenly purpose. The Process of being set aside from the world and its pleasures and systems and put to the task of playing our specific role in the Body of Christ is called sanctification and this is our preparation for ministry.

When Jesus was tested in the Wilderness, He defeated the Devil by the Holy Spirit. The Devil could not find anything within Jesus that he could use to get Him to respond out of the nature of the Flesh. The Devil has only one thing to work with in us; it is our Flesh. If it is dead, there is nothing for him to use to tempt and defeat us. Jesus was tested three times and three times He responded in the Spirit. Our sanctification is also our armor. It protects us from the deception and lure that the Devil uses to get us to respond to the desires of the Flesh. A pure Heart that is surrendered to God presumes nothing. The sanctified saint submits everything of importance to the direction and Lordship of Jesus. This surrender is not always an action, but is rather a Heart attitude of humility which depends on God for everything.

Thc Hcart Of Man

It is the Heart which is spirit and which has within it the capacity to know and love God. Because it is in the spirit realm that we interact with God and do our ministry, it is this part of us that is critical to our preparation for ministry. By being prepared, we are transformed on the spirit level so we can fully surrender to the Holy Spirit and overcome the Old Nature. This is fundamental to Christianity, but, as God prepares us, this is the point at which we "live" or die in the Wilderness. Being set aside fully for the Lord is the foundation, not only for our ministry, but for personal peace, joy, provision, authority, and the love which needs to be the motive for ministry. Without these qualities, we cannot be fruitful in ministry. There may well be a great deal of activity, but changing a Heart is a spiritual matter which can only be done Spirit to spirit. If love is not the motive, then the Spirit of God is not in the ministry, and it will not bear fruit. Fruitful ministry will last forever and can endure the test of God's consuming fire.

The human Heart is the window through which God can reach this world. He is Spirit and it is through our spirit He is manifested. The condition of our Heart, therefore, influences the purity of our ministry. Preparation for ministry is for the most part, the purging and preparation of the Heart.

When my daughter was three years old, she drew what I thought was a revealing picture of herself. It demonstrated that the essence of her being is spirit. The picture illustrates that we "live" out of our spirit, or Heart, and this is the point at which we touch, and are touched, by God.

The following is a selection of Scriptures about the Heart.

The Nature of the Heart

1. ***For as he thinketh in his heart, so [is] he:*** (Proverbs 23:7)

2. ***Above all else, guard your heart,*** *for it is the* ***wellspring of life.*** *Put away perversity from your mouth; keep corrupt talk far from your lips (Prov. 4:23-24)*

3. ***The sacrifices of God [are] a broken spirit: a broken and a contrite heart,*** *O God, thou wilt not despise.* (Psalms 51:17)

4. ***He that loveth pureness of heart,*** *[for]* ***the grace*** *of his lips the king [shall be] his friend.* (Proverbs 22:11)
5. ***A sound heart [is] the life of the flesh****: but envy the rottenness of the bones.* (Proverbs 14:30)

God Looks On the Heart

6. But the LORD said unto Samuel, Look not on his countenance, or on the height of his stature; because I have refused him: for [the LORD seeth] not as man seeth; for man looketh on the outward appearance, ***but the LORD looketh on the heart.*** (1 Samuel 16:7)
7. He that hath clean hands, and a ***pure heart****; who hath not lifted up his soul unto vanity, nor sworn deceitfully.* (Psalms 24:4)
8. Shall not God search this out? For ***he knoweth the secrets of the heart****.* (Psalms 44:21)

The Wickedness of the Heart

9. Thus saith the LORD; Cursed [be] the man that trusteth in man, and maketh flesh his arm, and ***whose heart departeth from the LORD..... The heart [is] deceitful above all [things], and desperately wicked: who can know it? I the LORD search the heart****, [I] try the reins, even to give every man according to his ways, [and] according to the fruit of his doings.* (Jeremiah 17:5-10)
10. The foolishness of man perverteth his way: and ***his heart fretteth against the LORD.*** (Proverbs 19:3)
11. And if he come to see [me], he speaketh vanity: ***his heart gathereth iniquity to itself;*** *[when] he goeth abroad, he telleth [it].* (Psalms 41:6)
12. When he speaketh fair, believe him not: ***for [there are] seven abominations in his heart.*** (Proverbs 26:25)
13. ***He that trusteth in his own heart is a fool****: but whoso walketh wisely, he shall be delivered.* (Proverbs 28:26)
14. This [is] an evil among all [things] that are done under the sun, that [there is] one event unto all: yea, also ***the heart of the sons of men is full of evil, and madness [is] in their heart*** *while they live,..* (Ecclesiastes 9:3)

15. Foolishness [is] bound in the heart of a child; [but] the rod of correction shall drive it far from him. (Proverbs 22:15)

God Cleanses the Heart
16. ***Create in me a clean heart****, O God; and renew a right spirit within me.* (Psalms 51:10)
17. And the LORD thy God will bring thee into the land which thy fathers possessed, and thou shalt possess it; and he will do thee good, and multiply thee above thy fathers. ***And the LORD thy God will circumcise thine heart, and the heart of thy seed,*** *to love the LORD thy God with all thine heart, and with all thy soul, that thou mayest live.* (Deuteronomy 30 5-6)
18. Circumcise yourselves to the LORD, and ***take away the foreskins of your heart,*** *ye men of Judah and inhabitants of Jerusalem: lest my fury come forth like fire, and burn that none can quench [it], because of the evil of your doings.* (Jeremiah 4:4)
19. ***I the LORD search the heart,*** *[I] try the reins, even to give* ***every man*** *according to his ways, [and] according to the fruit of his doings.* (Jeremiah 17:10)
20. And I will give ***them an heart to know me****, that I [am] the LORD: and they shall be my people, and I will be their God: for they shall return unto me with their* ***whole heart****.* (Jeremiah 24:7)

The Tree of the Knowledge of Good and Evil
The Adamic Nature is profiled in the story of the fall of man. A careful review of Adam and Eve's reactions to their sin reveals a clear picture of the ways and nature of the Old Man. If we can judge our own actions as Flesh or Spirit, we are better equipped to respond to the Spirit and destroy the works of the Flesh in our life.

Immediately upon eating of the Tree of the Knowledge of Good and Evil, the couple began to interact differently with God. The fall changed their view of Him. They hid themselves because they were afraid. On a deeper level than we can see without the revelation of the Holy Spirit, this fear of God is still alive in the unredeemed Heart. Outwardly, we may be praising the Lord, but inwardly, our relationship with God may be hindered by feelings which we neither understand or are prepared to acknowledge. Paul said that these feelings do not belong to us, but to the Old Man.

As it is, it is no longer I myself who do it, but it is sin living in me. Romans 7:17 NIV

The New Man has been resurrected in the Spirit, yet the Old Man is still alive. The battle for supremacy is both a battle of daily choice, and the redemptive work of the Holy Spirit. Therefore, we are freer today from the lusts of the Flesh (Old Man) than we were last year, but we must choose to live in that freedom every day.

When Adam and Eve ate of the fruit, they also became aware that they were naked and they covered up. This is one of the characteristics of the Adamic Nature. The Flesh will do whatever it can to cover or hide its sin or motives. By our very nature, we suppress our sin and deny it is there because we feel guilty and humbled when it is revealed. It is a characteristic of the Flesh to avoid looking at the truth. The Spirit exposes sin but the Flesh wants to hide it and condemn us. If we are deceived by the Flesh, we may cooperate with it to cover our sin instead of exposing it. As we experience the redemption of God, we develop a love and appreciation for the truth and how it can contribute to the quality of our life. We learn to love the truth, even when it exposes us. We learn from experience that the truth will set us free and there is peace in freedom. The suppression of our sin only serves to create inner turmoil. We were not created for sin. We are separated from the provision, safety, and fellowship of God, who is the only One who can tell us who we are. To know Christ and who we are in Him brings us to inner peace. It is impossible to estimate the damage stress caused by sin does when it weakens the body, torments the mind, and pains the emotions. Choosing truth and freedom is choosing life.

Another expression of the Adamic Nature was revealed by Adam when he blamed God for his sin. To paraphrase, he said, "*It was the woman that you gave me, who got me into this trouble*". Eve blamed the serpent. Both of them were acting true to their new fallen nature. The Adamic Nature will blame others, including God, for the consequences of its actions. When we become hurt because of our sin, we, at a Heart level even when it is not consciously known to us, will blame God for letting us be in pain. A sign of spiritual maturity and wholeness as a person is to acknowledge sin quickly and take it to God. It is the Flesh that demands that we "tip-toe" around it. It is our Sin Nature that is defensive, offended, or in denial. We need to be ruthless toward our sin, rise up in the Holy Spirit and take our Sin Nature to the cross. It is not a reflection of us (the New Man), but it is a reflection of the Old Man who we need to put to death and bury on a daily basis. The true measure of spiritual maturity is marked in the willingness to face sin head on. It requires a determined commitment to turn against it, instead of taking an offence. We must not deny our sin when we are confronted by the Holy Spirit's quest for Lordship of our life. This is a fundamental principle in growing up in God: to learn to turn against the works of the Flesh, even in the heat of the moment, and call upon the Spirit to rule in the situation. Every time we choose life in the Spirit, we take more ground in our Heart for the Kingdom of God, which will produce in us love, joy, and peace.

Unbelief

The Adamic Nature's most prevalent characteristic is unbelief. It is the least noticeable, but one of the "roots" of the nature. When the serpent tempted Eve, he suggested that maybe God was keeping something good from them, by forbidding them to eat of the Tree of the Knowledge of Good and Evil. Of course, this subtle suggestion was a lie about the character of God, but Eve believed it, and ate. The root of much of our sin can be traced back to what we don't believe about God. If we believe that God doesn't care about us or that He will help others, but He will not help us in a particular area, then we are in unbelief about the character of God. The Children of Israel died in the Wilderness because they believed the lie of the Adamic Nature and would not believe that what the Holy Spirit had done for them in the past, He would do again. God is not partial toward anyone and what He has done for others He will do for you, IF you believe Him. Subtle as it may be, much of our sin against God is rooted in our unbelief. Faith and belief are Heart issues. Faith is spiritual. It straddles this world and the spiritual world. It is the conduit through which God moves His provision from the spiritual world into the temporal world. Faith is the product of the redeemed Heart.

When the unfaithful servant returned the talents to his master, he said, "*He knew Him to be a hard man*" (Matt 25:24). The Master did not correct his distorted view of Him. He was not unreasonably demanding (hard) with the second servant who did not produce as much return as the first servant. The unfaithful servant's perception of the Master put him in fear, which kept him from doing what was reasonably prudent with the talents (giftings) he had been given. His fear paralysed him and brought on exactly what he feared - the wrath of the Master. Fear is the direct result of unbelief. If we know who God is and that nothing can separate us from His love, then there is nothing in life to fear. Fear produces striving, ongoing anxiety, manipulation of situations, and attempts to find replacements for the relationship we would have if we were not separated from God by our sin of unbelief. When we get a revelation of God and His love for us, it brings us to a peace that transcends any circumstance. When we see His power and ability to provide, and to protect, and His love for us, we are secure and at rest, even in the middle of a figurative or literal battlefield. Pride is the result of not knowing who we are because we do not know who God is. If the God of the Universe loves us in our fallen pathetic state, then we must be important to Him. We don't have to strive for anything because in Him there is everything we need. Nothing this world has to offer could be more than what we already have in our relationship with the Father, Son, and Holy Spirit. He is our supply, our defender, our joy, and our happiness. In Him is found everything to make life full and abundantly fulfilling. If we don't believe that, we will be faced with making ourselves happy, which will lead to folly and idolatry.

The Tree of The Knowledge of Good and Evil

Suicide
Murder
Self hate
Hatred
Drunkeness
Jealousy
Deception
Witchcraft
Dissipation
Driven
Promiscuity
Lust
Aggression
Greed
Bitterness
Materialism
Shyness
Unloved
Self-Reliance
Confusion
Rebellion
Pride
Anger
Manipulation
Insecurity
Ambition
FEAR
IDOLATRY
IMPURE MOTIVES
UNBELIEF

The Adamic Nature

Summary

The Heart is the spirit of man. It is the dimension which touches and is touched by God. The state of the Heart is the determining factor in our relationship with God and our fruitfulness in ministry. The Heart is the deepest level of our being which we rarely see, except by the revelation of the Holy Spirit; yet it controls our life. "*.... guard your heart, for it is the wellspring of life.*" (Proverbs 4:23). Without faith, we cannot please God, yet our very nature is to be unbelieving. Therefore, the purity of Heart that we attain will enable us to hear God and do His will and please Him. Our faith in God's character as a loving Father, at the Heart level, is what brings pleasure and glory to Him. The summation of all of the law is to love God with all of your Heart, mind, and strength and your neighbour as yourself. Therefore, it is our goal as Christians to be sanctified and fully able to walk, surrendered to the Holy Spirit. In that, we will achieve our calling and bring glory to God because we will overcome the Flesh, the Devil, and the world.

What we have of God in the way of knowledge and understanding is but a crumb of the eternal feast of heavenly treasures that is available in Him. It may take us ten or twenty years of walking with Him before the impact of this truth sets into our life. We could spend the rest of our lifetime and all of eternity pursuing the riches of Him, and we would never exhaust the joy of discovering all there is in our Father God. We know this, but for the most part, we don't live our lives as if it were true. The greatest joy and pleasures in this life are not the respect or honour of men, nor is it the material comforts of this life. ALL the real treasure is in Him. The average Christian will say "*amen*" to that, but it isn't where he lives. Unbelievers and the unchurched Believers can see through the hypocrisy of the Church. If it is true that Jesus is coming back for His Bride, why do we live as though there are a million tomorrows? If He will judge the living and the dead, why do we live with one foot in the world and one in the Kingdom? It is because we are not free to walk in the Spirit. We are like Paul wanting to do better, but failing miserably (Romans 7:23-24). Our enemies are much stronger than ourselves. The Flesh can only be defeated by our God. The Flesh is still alive in us. Romans is a picture of the battle between the Old Man and the New. We have put on the New Man but as is the case with salvation, we are saved and being saved. We are New and being made New (Col. 3). Paul goes on to give us a beautifully clear view of how we should look at this battle which rages within us. He explains:

Now if I do what I do not want to do, it is no longer I who do it, but it is sin living in me that does it. Romans 7:20 NIV

We have been redeemed, and are whole and fully redeemed in the eyes of our Lord. It is not us who sins, but it is the Old Man or sin which does these things. We are the New Man, but there lives also in us the Old Man. We know truth but we can't and don't live it because the enemy of the Holy Spirit is also alive in us. There is no condemnation in Christ Jesus. We are saved from our duplicity by grace. We are saved by grace and need to continue to seek the grace which saves us from our enemy, the Flesh. Our choices are what determine who will reign over us. The purpose of the Wilderness is to put us in a dependent relationship with God our provider. The more we see Him, the easier it is to choose and believe in His goodness even when we are in need. The more we choose Him, the greater the power that is given to the New Man in our life and the more we weaken the Old Man.

Chapter Four

Why The Wilderness?

See, I have refined you, though not as silver; I have tested you in the furnace of affliction. For my own sake, for my own sake, I do this. How can I let myself be defamed? I will not yield my glory to another. Isa. 48:10-11

When we were born again, we were transformed from the Old Man into the Spirit Man. This is symbolized by baptism. The previous chapter gives a brief overview of the state of man's Heart prior to God's sanctification. If Paul, in Romans 7, was still subject to falling victim to the Old Man after all he suffered, then how much more are we subject to the lusts of the Flesh? The above Scripture is one indication why God tests and sanctifies Believers. He will not allow His people to take the credit for what He is doing through them. Yet, if we are like Paul, unable to refrain from giving in to the Flesh, then only by grace are we able to do ministry without taking the glory. Of course, to acquire grace in the Kingdom, we must be humble.

It is not popular to preach suffering and humility, since that is not "seeker sensitive". We have many methods and gimmicks for making the Church successful, because it is success we believe to be our goal, but this kind of success is the desire of the Flesh. Success is God's responsibility. Our objective should be to walk obedient to the Spirit, wherever that might take us. This is the success which produces treasure in Heaven. It could look like failure on earth. Jesus' ministry was a spiritual success, even though in the natural He would appear to have been a loser of losers. Our ministry should not be judged in the natural either. It is in the spirit realm and it takes faith to invest our life in that which cannot be seen with human eyes. Unfortunately, many of our objectives and ministry goals are carnal, because tangible, successful ministry makes us look good. At the root of our motive is the Flesh, not the Spirit, and that kind of ministry will not bear eternal fruit for the Kingdom, but will be burned up at the end of the Age. Paul warned us of this, because it is so easy to fall into. (1 Cor. 3:12-15)

For Believers whose objective it is to walk in the Spirit, the Flesh is our main opponent, yet in the Church, we rarely even mention it. We condemn the outward expressions of the Flesh such as sexual immorality, or foul language, but we tolerate the sins of the Heart, such as greed, materialism, and ambition. They are tolerated in the Church, sometimes even revered. Most Churches are trying to meet their budget or expand into new ministry. They cannot financially afford to offend people by exposing and confronting the Flesh. Their ministry goals lead them to compromises which accommodate the Flesh. The irony is that ministry should be the war against the Flesh. The Church, therefore, cannot effectively preach against the Flesh. It becomes a house divided against itself. Unless we are redeemed from our compromises and duplicity which we were born into, we will not stand. The Lord knows we are helpless to change ourselves. The Flesh is an enemy much bigger than we are. His intention is not to condemn us with our failings but to redeem us from our enemies. He will change us if we ask Him.

Jesus Is The Living Word

Jesus described Himself in Scripture as, "*the Way, the Truth, and the Life*". On other occasions He is described as the "Living Word". This is an accurate statement about our Lord, since He is the essence of truth. It is part of His being. He not only knows it, He IS the truth. Truth and Jesus are one. They cannot be separated, nor can we get truth from Him without taking Him. We can't separate Him from His salvation from sin. We can't separate Him from being the Abundant Life. He is all these things. **They are part** of Him because He humbled Himself and gave up His life on the cross. It was His suffering and humility and death that granted Him the title of: "the Way, the Truth, and the Life". If we are to be like Him, we must take up our cross and experience the death of our Flesh. Then we will find the Way, the Truth, and Life.

Can you remember the sermon you heard on Christmas 1997 or Easter 1995? Now try to remember the personal discipline of the Lord. Remember those illustrated sermons by the Holy Spirit or the time when He guided you, directed you, or convicted you. We learn by experience much better than by words. We go through this Process because it must be experienced rather than learned. It is in the experience of the Process we are transformed. Teaching tells us what we must do to interact and cooperate with the Spirit. But the work of Holy Spirit is done in walking with Him through experiences He prepares for us. Prophetic revelation is wonderful, but it doesn't change our Heart. It usually comes as a forerunner to the Holy Spirit working that truth into our Heart. As much as we would like to avoid the difficulties of the Process, there is no other way to have the character and treasure of the Kingdom developed in our lives.

If we suffer, we shall also reign with him: if we deny him, he also will deny us: 2 Tim. 2:12 NIV

The more we become like Christ, the more we can expect to suffer. If we believe that the world is operating in the Flesh, and the Holy Spirit and Flesh are at enmity with each other, then we can expect to be persecuted by the works of the Flesh inside and outside the Church. The irony is that suffering makes us more like Christ, and the more we are like Christ, the more the Flesh will attack us. Therefore, the more we suffer, the more we suffer. There is no other way to produce the fruit of the Holy Spirit and to have fruitful ministry. The less we suffer, the less we will become like Christ.

Walking In The Spirit

There is a specific period of time in which God prepares us with grace and reveals our call and the truth which is the basis for our "life message". The more we surrender to the Holy Spirit, the more He will lead us into suffering. The more suffering we experience, the more dead the Old Man becomes, and the stronger the Holy Spirit is alive in us. Jesus, our perfect example, said, "*I do only what I see the Father do.*" He had a revelation of the Father and did only what He saw Him doing. Jesus is our example. If we walk in the Holy Spirit, then we cannot fail in ministry or in our call. That does not mean we will not look like a failure, but when the books are opened at Judgement Day, they will reveal success. We will have treasure in Heaven because we have chosen to allow the Holy Spirit to be Lord of our life and He cannot fail. Our objective as New Testament, end-time, born-again, Spirit-filled Believers is to completely surrender in everything to the Holy Spirit. We are not called to know more, or to do more. We are called to walk in the Spirit because in this way we will follow Jesus' example to surrender His life to His Father, day by day, hour by hour. To walk in the Spirit as Jesus did required Him to completely put the Sin Man under the authority of the Holy Spirit. He moved forward only when the Spirit commanded. He did nothing without the Spirit's prompting. That is humility. That is surrender. That is death of self, and that is the way to powerful ministry. We must learn to walk in the Spirit.

Jesus said, "*Greater things you will do*" (John 14:12). Why would He say that? His vision of the end times was of a sanctified Church, which was surrendered to the Holy Spirit, demonstrating the power and authority of God over all things. It is His intention to reveal the Father through our love for one another and through spiritual power, manifested in the Church. This is a "greater thing" in that it will not be through only one person (Jesus), but through millions of people (the Church) who are like Jesus. Jesus had a huge impact on the world when He ministered here. How much more will the Church have when it is ministering in full surrender to the Holy Spirit?

God's Process of putting the Adamic Nature to death (sanctification) will allow us to walk in the Spirit. We will become like little children who are completely dependent on the Holy Spirit for everything. The Process will strip us of anything that the Flesh can use to fulfill itself, and in that way, we will learn to depend on the Holy Spirit. The things we suffer (the stripping away) teaches us to be obedient to the Holy Spirit. We learn that the works of the Flesh will not fulfill us and do not bring life, but death. When we walk in the Spirit, we minister life to a dead and dying world.

To be sanctified unto Jesus Christ is to be ruined for God. The more we become like Jesus, the more alienated we are to the world. To be ruined for God is to be a failure to this world, but a success in the Kingdom of God.

The more we suffer, the greater the vessel we are for grace. The world and the Church don't need more truth, they need more grace. We have the Scriptures, but can we live up to their high standard? We need more grace in order to live in the truth. The way to a dynamic and powerful Church and ministry is to have more grace, and that means humbling and suffering.

Real spiritual ministry requires us to own the truth that we are ministering. We must humble ourselves and through humility gain the grace to acquire the truth that we are called to minister. We can't produce in others the things we only know. How could an unbeliever lead another unbeliever to Christ? It would be the blind leading the blind. We can only bring to people the truths that we have acquired for ourselves. We acquire grace through humbling and when we have that truth we can minister it. If, as the Church, we are preaching only theories and truth without grace, we are like the Pharisees whom Jesus condemned and called blind men leading blind men. We become like a clanging gong when we espouse theology instead of Christ crucified. A seed cannot reproduce another seed. It must first go into the ground and die, then germinate to produce a small stalk, then a larger plant, then fruit which holds within it the seed. It is a process of growing toward fruitfulness. Our testimony is the most powerful thing we have in ministry, since it is an account of the grace and truth we have acquired. These are the truths which we can **impart** to others because we are in possession of them. It is through suffering and humility we acquire the truth of the Kingdom. God sanctifies us so that we will be fruitful ministers of the Gospel. When we know His humbling, we will know His grace, and then His truth.

For everyone who exalts himself will be humbled, and he who humbles himself will be exalted." Luke 14 :11 NIV

The Promised Land

The Children of Israel were promised a land filled with milk and honey. We are promised the riches of Christ found in His Kingdom. The riches are more fulfilling and wonderful than anything we could imagine with the carnal mind. God sanctifies us so we can enter into the promises and provision of the Father to us as Believers. Sanctification is the path to provision and the promises He has made to us in the Gospel, but these are nothing compared to knowing Jesus Christ. With each provision, each promise fulfilled, comes a further knowing and being like Jesus Christ. These are imperishable gifts which we will take with us into eternity.

Moses spent 40 years in his personal wilderness and emerged the humblest man on earth. He had endured the process of sanctification which the Lord prepared for him. Even then, He did not enter the Promised Land. The Apostle Paul was conscious of the risk of losing all that he had gained when he wrote;

Do you not know that in a race all the runners run, but only one gets the prize? Run in such a way as to get the prize. Everyone who competes in the games goes into strict training. They do it to get a crown that will not last; but we do it to get a crown that will last for ever. Therefore I do not run like a man running aimlessly; I do not fight like a man beating the air. No, I beat my body and make it my slave so that after I have preached to others, I myself will not be disqualified for the prize. 1 Cor. 9:24-27 NIV

To walk with God is a wonderful thing, but it is also a fearful thing. Paul was fully aware that should he ever begin to depend on himself, he would have lost some of what he had gained, and possibly been disqualified personally from the reward. He was aware that it was a daily choice to surrender to the Holy Spirit, even after He had suffered and acquired great riches in Christ. No matter what we gain in Christ, it never means we have "arrived", or that now we can relax. Sanctification only gives us the ability to live for God, but the choice is ours every day.

Our preparation will enable us to fully surrender to the Holy Spirit and to walk more completely in Him. Our suffering will bring forth treasures of the Kingdom and the grace to minister them to others. If there is going to be an acceleration of the preparation and empowering of the Church, it will be because the Holy Spirit will set aside a group of warriors such as Gideon's army who were not afraid. They will have the full armor of God and the grace to win victories over nations far more powerful than themselves. They will be a people of faith who have been purged of the demands of the Old Man and the Flesh, and who love God with all of their Heart, mind, and strength. *For many are invited, but few are chosen.* Matt. 22:14 NIV

Chapter Five

The Allegory Of The Children of Israel

For I do not want you to be ignorant of the fact, brothers, that our forefathers were all under the cloud and that they all passed through the sea. They were all baptised into Moses in the cloud and in the sea. They all ate the same spiritual food and drank the same spiritual drink; for they drank from the spiritual rock that accompanied them, and that rock was Christ. Nevertheless, God was not pleased with most of them; their bodies were scattered over the desert. ***Now these things occurred as examples to keep us from setting our hearts on evil things as they did.*** *Do not be idolaters, as some of them were; as it is written: "The people sat down to eat and drink and got up to indulge in pagan revelry." We should not commit sexual immorality, as some of them did— and in one day twenty-three thousand of them died. We should not test the Lord, as some of them did—and were killed by snakes. And do not grumble, as some of them did—and were killed by the destroying angel.* ***These things happened to them as examples and were written down as warnings for us, on whom the fulfilment of the ages has come.*** 1 Cor. 10:1-11 NIV

The Children of Israel's deliverance from bondage in Egypt is by far the most detailed account of any time in the history of God's people. In some cases, the Scripture account was written on a daily basis with many details about what happened on a number of fronts. All of this detail has a purpose. It has been accurately maintained for close to 5000 years as 1 Cor. 10:11 says, "for our warning". The New American Standard version translates "warning" as "for our instruction". Based on this and the fact that even David gave an account of the deliverance of Israel from Egypt in the Psalms, God has underscored to us the importance of this story for our welfare and understanding. If this story is for our instruction, then it is more than just the deliverance of God's people from an oppressive situation, but a demonstration of **how** God delivers His people. It is an allegory for our own deliverance and a warning for us to not react to God's ways, as Israel did.

Consider that God planned and executed the deliverance of the Children of Israel in a detailed way. Scripture says that God hardened Pharaoh's Heart to show the surrounding nations that He was Israel's God. He proved to the Children of Israel and to Moses that He would defend them and provide for them in supernatural ways. God knew exactly what He would do with them and where he was taking them. He knew exactly how He would defeat the nations that would oppose them. Everything in the story was predetermined to be just the way it happened. The only thing that was not predetermined was the Children of Israel's failure to follow God in faith. It is clear that the recording of all the detail was designed with a purpose. The story is an allegory, but also a paradigm of the methods God used and the purposes He had at every stage in the Children of Israel's journey. Their Wilderness experience says as much about God as it does about Israel. His plan was concise and purposeful in every detail. He arranged every circumstance for a specific reason. He hardened Pharaoh's Heart. He had the Egyptian Army attack when Israel was at the Red Sea. He had them run out of water, then provided water from the Rock, and so on. Each event in the story was planned by God for us to read and learn from today. That is what 1 Cor. 10 says.

From this story of the Children of Israel, we are to learn what God's purposes are, what His ways are, and what we should and should not do. Specifically, the story warns us to cooperate with God in the Wilderness, and not to rebel against the discipline and purging of the Process. The lesson teaches us the way God sanctifies His people, and in that, to not rebel against His hand of discipline and purging.

The Children of Israel were promised a land filled with milk and honey. They were promised vineyards they did not plant, cities they did not build. They were warned that when they came into the fullness of the promise, they must not think they had achieved this by the power of their own hand. This is a picture of grace. The Promised Land is a place of grace for the New Testament Believer. It is a place of being and doing, with the emphasis on being. The Promised Land was not only a place of abundance, but also a place of peace. There would be no war. The enemies of Israel were put to rest by God himself. Peace, to a people who had been fighting for decades inside the Promised Land was very important and appealing. The Kingdom of God is characterized by peace. Jesus is called "The Prince of Peace". For the Believer, the Promised Land is a place of peace and rest. The Kingdom of God is not about physical things, although it has effect on the physical dimension, but it is a place of spiritual peace. Our enemies, which are the works of the Flesh, will be put under the authority of the Holy Spirit. The abundant provision is also a spiritual abundance as well: intimacy and fullness, contentment and knowledge of God.

So the LORD gave Israel all the land he had sworn to give their forefathers, and they took possession of it and settled there. The LORD gave them rest on every side, just as he had sworn to their forefathers. Not one of their enemies withstood them; the LORD handed all their enemies over to them. Not one of all the LORD's good promises to the house of Israel failed; every one was fulfilled.
Joshua 21:43-45 NIV

The Promised Land was also a place of bringing glory to God. The very fact that God's people trusted Him and faithfully obeyed Him, even when they didn't understand what He was doing, was pleasing to God. Israel did what God told them to do, and because of that, He was able to overcome their enemies for them. He had a people through whom He could express His love, His ways, and His power. This brings glory to God. It also revealed Him as God of Heaven and earth, and left a witness in Scripture for generations to come. Israel, during much of the taking of the Land, was faithful and God proved to be faithful to them. He gave them the Levitical Law which outlined the principles of modern day hygiene and which saved them from disease and epidemics. He taught them the principles of spiritual law so they would live a fruitful and emotionally peaceful life. His intention was to bless Israel and to show the nations of the world that in Him there is blessing. By following Him, they had an abundance of blessing on all levels of life. Hebrews 8:4-7 says that the Old Covenant is a shadow, or pattern, for the New Covenant Church. God is going to write His law on the Hearts of His people. He is going to circumcise our Hearts, which means to set us apart, as a people who are wholly His. Those people who have been circumcised of Heart will be guided by the Holy Spirit and have the authority and power of God within them. They will be victorious in the Spirit realm, defeating the enemies of God and taking rulership over the earth. God's purpose is to have a people who will be obedient to the Holy Spirit, so He can bring them into blessings that have never before been known.

However, as it is written: "No eye has seen, no ear has heard, no mind has conceived what God has prepared for those who love him"— but God has revealed it to us by his Spirit. 1 Cor. 2:9-10 NIV

Each stage in the Children of Israel's journey is a stage in God's refining process of setting us aside as wholly unto the Lord. Each step in the journey is meant to bring us to greater humility and surrender to the Holy Spirit. The journey from Egypt to the Promised Land chronicles the systematic process that God uses to prepare us for our ministry of being and doing. He reveals this Process to His people so that we will cooperate with it, and not rebel, as the first generation of Israelites did. Understanding this Process is of importance since we will probably never enter the promises or the fulfillment of our call without understanding the process of preparation. Israel perished in the Wilderness without knowing the victory or the fullness of provision that God had planned for them. They were delivered powerfully from Egypt. They saw the miracles of the plagues. They plundered the Egyptians of their gold, silver, and fine clothing. They even saw God part the Red Sea on their behalf. They received water out of the Rock and were fed manna in the Wilderness, but they were still far from possessing what God had in store for them. The Promised Land was much more than that. We may be content with some healing and some spiritual manna from time to time, but there is so much more that the Lord has prepared for us. We have been promised by Jesus, that we would do greater things than what He did (John 14:12). We have been promised the power to raise up and pull down kingdoms, to raise the dead, and to heal every sickness. We have been promised love, joy, peace, and provision from God for every need. We will be like Him and rule the Universe with Him. These promises are conditional upon our obedience to Him, just as they were with Israel. The restoration of the Church to wholeness will produce an interdependent, unified force on the face of the earth which will conquer the opponents of God, the Flesh, and the Powers of Darkness and set men free. The Church will also be known for its love between its members.

The Church is being lead into the Wilderness by the Holy Spirit. He is drawing those called of Him to follow Him. Some have entered the Process, but have run aground on the shoals of bitterness, unbelief, and rebellion. Some of the Church have given up on their call and have turned back looking for a place of comfort, even if it is not the freedom and blessing they were promised. If you are feeling that the Spirit is beckoning you to get back to walking with Him. Do not refuse His call!

Like any Bride who is preparing for a wedding, she may be somewhat disarrayed as she is being readied, but this disarray is only on the outside. We, the Bride of Christ, may appear to be in total disarray as the Holy Spirit prepares us for Jesus, but fine gold will be the result of His work. The time of preparation for Jesus' return and the beginning of a New Age will bring turmoil to both the world and the Church. The true Church will be strengthened by the turmoil, not swept away by it. It will literally thrive on the persecution and the de-stabilization of the world's systems which will happen just before the appearance of the Anti-christ. These things will only serve to further purify the Church. What is Flesh will collapse, but what is Spirit will endure forever. Those who are prepared will not be washed away by the coming turmoil. The sanctified Church will not look like the Church of today. It will be more zealous and passionate. God will purify the Hearts of His people, so He can pour His power through them without destroying their lives. He would never risk losing one of His children to prove who He is to the world. This purity of Heart will protect us from "blowing up" in spiritual pride when God does dramatic and powerful things through us. Our surrender and humility will be entrusted with power and authority so He will get the glory.

The Journey by the Children of Israel has three distinct stages to it. In each of these stages, God deals with a different area of the Believer's Adamic Nature. These stages are: the Wilderness, Jericho, and the defeat of the Seven Nations. In each of these stages, God had a specific purpose in mind when redeeming Israel. The following three chapters are dedicated to understanding the process, the stages, the steps, and God's purposes and ways, so we can better respond to the preparation He has prescribed for us.

Chapter Six

Stage One: The Wilderness

And Jesus being full of the Holy Ghost returned from Jordan, and was led by the Spirit into the wilderness, Being forty days tempted of the devil. And in those days he did eat nothing: and when they were ended, he afterward hungered. And the devil said unto him, if thou be the Son of God, command this stone that it be made bread. And Jesus answered him, saying, It is written, That man shall not live by bread alone, but by every word of God. Luke 4:1-4

Moses spent 40 years in the Wilderness. Jesus spent 40 days fasting and praying and being tested by the Devil in the Wilderness. In Jesus' case, there was nothing of the Flesh found in Him. Verse 14 of Luke 4 says that after He came out of the desert, He returned to Galilee "in the power of the Spirit" and news about Him spread through all the surrounding districts. This was the beginning of His public ministry. Scripture records that He was tempted by the Devil three times. The first temptation which corresponds to the first stage of this Process (the Wilderness) relates to His surrender to the Holy Spirit. It was the Holy Spirit who had lead Him into the Wilderness where there was no food. Jesus was willing to stay there until the Holy Spirit gave Him permission to leave the desert. The Devil tempted Him to provide for His needs by his own hand and turn the stones into bread. Jesus responded by quoting Deut. 8:3, "*man shall not live by bread alone, but by every word which proceeds out of the mouth of God.*" Jesus was saying that the very purpose of the Wilderness is to humble the Believer and that the experience of the Wilderness was meant to teach submission to the Holy Spirit. God let Israel become hungry and remain in need to humble them. He was teaching them that they were helpless, and must completely surrender to the Father. They were to learn to wait on the Lord and not rebel by providing for themsclvcs. They needed to learn not to complain but remain in faith about God's love for them in spite of their need. These are lessons learned through the experience of the Wilderness. It is in need and humble circumstances that the Holy Spirit transforms and makes complete surrender and trust of the Father a part of our life. Life experiences truly change us. Being hungry and being humbled are painful at the time, but they are part of the maturing of every Believer. It is God's process of integrating truth into our life. For the Children of Israel and for Jesus, the Wilderness was a physical place; however, for us as New Covenant Children of God, the Wilderness is a place of spiritual barrenness and difficult circumstances. The way God works to bring new truth to His people is to first bring it by revelation and thereby create the desire for this truth to become a reality in our life. He then begins a process of bringing the Flesh to the cross and resurrecting the Spirit Man in this specific area of our life, so we can live in the truth. This Process has been described as getting the truth to travel the twelve inches from our head to our Heart. It isn't far, but it is quite a journey.

God has spoken promises to His people and those words are alive and will bring provision, deliverance, and life. We cannot live as Christians without hearing and experiencing the presence of the Holy Spirit. The Children of Israel had a cloud with them by day and a pillar of fire at night. They knew their God was with them. Life for the Christian must be surrendered and lead by the Holy Spirit or it is an empty existence of wandering aimlessly in life. Even if we know how to pray and trust God for our needs and are not being lead day by day, we are walking in some form of rebellion in our Christian walk. The Christian life is a journey and only the Holy Spirit knows the way. If we are not following Him, then we are rebels in the Wilderness. If it weren't for "our Moses" Jesus, who sits at the right hand of God and intercedes for us, we would be cut off in the Wilderness as the first generation of the Children of Israel were. We would never have a chance to live in the full blessing and peace of God, except by His grace. When we are following the Holy Spirit, it is the most exciting adventure any person could live. He promises to make us victorious over our enemies and to do exploits which are far beyond our own ability. Without a vision for our life, we are only waiting to perish. But as surrendered followers of the Holy Spirit, we will know purpose, passion, and the treasures of the Kingdom.

The second purpose of the Wilderness, as stated in Deut. 8, was to test God's people. The Wilderness is a dry and wearying place. It is a place of need. It is hot. It is a place where survival is the only focus. It is a place of pressure, emptiness, and death of vision. At best, it is just an existence. The Wilderness is a big place. It can go on and on for hundreds of miles. It is a place where we can't see anything, except more desert. It is death of everything God has promised us. It tests our faith in God to provide and to fulfill His promise of abundance and fruitfulness. Week after week, month after month, and year after year, there is nothing but emptiness and need. The circumstances may be financial, or medical, or some other "chronic condition". No matter what the specific circumstances, they cause us to suffer. They become anguish to our soul. We know and believe God can deliver us in a heartbeat, but He doesn't, and that is the test. When we are pressed on from all sides, will we believe that God still loves us, or will we rebel against Him?

The rebellion can be so subtle. It may be a seemingly harmless indulgence to soothe ourselves "*when no one cares*". Our rebellion may be more overt and come in the form of taking control of the situation. Rationale like "*God doesn't want us to suffer*" is true in general, but without the light of the Holy Spirit in the situation, we may be fighting against God. Only the Holy Spirit can be our guide in the Wilderness. There are times when suffering is the work of the Holy Spirit in our lives. It is easy to justify making a "place" for the Flesh if wc do not see with Spiritual eyes the purpose God has for the situation. Jesus did not take His life into His own hands by turning the stones into bread. He waited for the Holy Spirit to tell Him it was time to leave the Wilderness regardless of how uncomfortable it was. He continued to believe in the goodness of His Father. He surrendered to His Lordship and acted in faith by agreeing with, and proclaiming the Scriptures (God's word) for His situation.

The Children of Israel didn't understand God's purposes or why He allowed their needs to be so severe. Had they understood His ways and His purposes, they may not have grumbled and rebelled, but rather turned their energies toward searching their Hearts for their unbelief. The only way to survive the Wilderness is to constantly reaffirm to ourselves the loving kindness of God and our need to be sanctified. Putting the Old Man to death is not an easy job, but our God is like a skilled surgeon. Secondly, we must turn against our Hearts and ask the Holy Spirit to expose what unbelief is present in us, then confess it and allow God to bring these areas to death. There is no substitute for living through this Process over a period of timc. Thc dcstination is a product of the journey. However, if we cooperate with the Holy Spirit, understanding God's purposes and ways, we are less likely to rebel against His refining and more likely to minimize the time we spend working through this stage of the Process.

Some time later God tested Abraham. He said to him. "Abraham" "Here I am, " he replied. Then God said, "Take your son, your only son, Isaac, whom you love, and go to the region of Moriah. Sacrifice him there as a burnt offering on one of the mountains I will tell you about." Early the next morning Abraham got up and saddled his donkey. He took with him two of his servants and his son Isaac. When he had cut enough wood for the burnt offering, he set out for the place God had told him about.

On the third day Abraham looked up and saw the place in the distance. He said to his servants, "Stay here with the donkey while I and the boy go over there. We will worship and then we will come back to you." Abraham took the wood for the burnt offering and placed it on his son Isaac, and he himself carried the fire and the knife. As the two of them went on together, Isaac spoke up and said to his father Abraham. "Father?" "Yes, my son?" Abraham replied. "The fire and wood are here," Isaac said, "but where is the lamb for the burnt offering?" Abraham answered, "God himself will provide the lamb for the burnt offering, my son." And the two of them went on together. When they reached the place God had told him about, Abraham built an altar there and arranged the wood on it. He bound his son Isaac and laid him on the altar, on top of the wood. Then he reached out his hand and took the knife to slay his son. But the angel of the LORD called out to him from heaven. 'Abraham Abraham" "Here I am," he replied. "Do not lay a hand on the boy," he said. "Do not do anything to him. Now I know that you fear God, because you have not withheld from me your son, your only son." Abraham looked up and there in a thicket he saw a ram caught by its horns. He went over and took the ram and sacrificed it as a burnt offering instead of his son. So Abraham called that place The LORD Will Provide." Gen. 22:1-14 NIV

The story of Abraham and Isaac has always fascinated me. Whenever I have heard it taught, it has been from the perspective of Abraham. For some reason, I thought it interesting to look at the story from Isaac's perspective. He was a young lad, probably about twelve or thirteen years old, when God told Abraham to sacrifice him. Isaac completely trusted his father. Even though there was no lamb for the sacrifice, which was quite unusual, Isaac trusted and never perceived that he would be harmed by his father. He was laid upon the altar and with love in his father's eyes, the knife was raised to sacrifice him. We don't know all the details,

Scripture leaves them unclear, but I always imagined a trusting child, looking into the eyes of his loving father, who even then did not attempt to escape or distrust the love which he knew his father had for him. When we are on the altar of "self" sacrifice and we feel the cold blade of imminent destruction, we must look into the Father's loving eyes and trust that nothing can separate us from His love. He loves us and means us no harm. His only purpose is to test, expose, and redeem us from the tyranny of our lusting Heart. God tested Abraham on the mountain, but he tested Isaac as well. When the angel of the Lord appeared and spared Isaac, he also provided a ram for the sacrifice. Then Abraham called that place, "*The Lord will Provide*".

Our Promise Of Provision

Abraham was able to respond to God in obedience because he knew Him. He understood that God was both loving and kind and that no matter what the outcome of the sacrifice, God would still fulfill His promise. Abraham took no ownership in what God had promised He would do through him. He left it up to God to accomplish, in His way. He did not try to second guess Him, nor argue that perhaps He was making a mistake by killing Isaac. He operated in faith, trusting the Father. Sometimes, when God tests us we are able to respond in faith; sometimes when God tests us, it is to expose our unbelief. However, if we see our sin in a situation and quickly call upon the Lord to deliver us, we can turn a failure into a victory. Every situation that comes our way is for a purpose. Either we respond to it in faith or we respond to it in fear. If we respond in faith, then the situation has been provided for the glory of God. If we respond to it in fear, and we can see ourselves in the circumstances, we can turn it into an opportunity to allow God to change us.

I was praying for someone on one occasion and the Lord gave me a vision. I was looking down on a large wooden square with many pigeon holes (smaller boxes) in the square. In some of the small boxes there was light shining through and in some of these boxes there was no light shining through at all. When I inquired of the Lord what this meant, He explained that the larger box represented the man's Heart. The smaller pigeon hole boxes were the various areas of his life. In some areas he was able to operate in faith (grace), and in other areas there was no light shining through at all. There was sin keeping him from the blessing that God wanted to bring to his life. Each of these areas God wanted to redeem so the man could enter into all the promises, but a lack of understanding of the ways and purposes of God were hindering the Holy Spirit's work. The man's lack of trust in the Father also prevented him from responding to God in faith, instead of rebelling against Him. He had God judged as an ogre with a big stick who was keeping him from the "good" things in life. The man did not see that the treasures of the Kingdom are of far greater value than anything that the world has to offer. Righteousness, peace, love, joy, grace, intimacy, spiritual abundance have the capacity to fulfill us beyond our wildest and most extreme expectations. What the world and the Flesh offer is pathetic by comparison. In order to respond to God correctly, we must believe that God is good, not just in our head, but in our Heart.

I can't speak for God, but I can speculate that even if we don't always respond correctly, He is not offended, as long as we don't shut down communication and turn against Him. If we shut down communication and lock Him out of our life by our judgment of Him, we become "shipwrecked" in the Wilderness. We run aground and cannot move forward. We, without sustenance, have cut off our only source of life in the Wilderness. Our old life becomes just a mirage on the horizon behind us. What was once there, is there no longer. We cannot go back to the way things used to be. They don't exist any more. We must either go forward or dry up spiritually in the desert. There are no other choices for us, just as there was no other choice for Israel.

"Let the nations be roused; let them advance into the Valley of Jehoshaphat there I will sit to judge all the nations on every side. Swing the sickle, for the harvest is ripe. Come, trample the grapes, for the winepress is full and the vats overflow so great is their wickedness." Multitudes, multitudes in the valley of decision. For the day of the LORD is near in the valley of decision. Joel 3:12-14

God is taking a great risk with us by driving us into the Wilderness. Yet for Him there is no other way. He will prepare a Bride who is spotless and pure. Some will be sanctified and others will not survive the journey. "*Many are called but few are chosen*". Matt. 22:14

Rebellion and Coping in the Wilderness

One of the most powerful tools we have been given as human beings is the power to choose. As with all of God's gifts to man, we can use it for good or for evil. When God called the Children of Israel a rebellious people, He was making a statement about their spiritual condition. They did not know Him. The Wilderness, in itself, is designed to put us in intimate contact with our Provider. The circumstances may be the loss of a job, being falsely accused, illness, or other unpleasant situations of need which are beyond our control. The Wilderness is not a situation which is the result of our own sinful or unwise action. The Wilderness is also not a bad week, or even a bad month at work. It is a season of life characterized by a dryness of spirit and difficult circumstances.

Our reaction to the circumstances which God chooses for us will either draw us to Him or cause us to rebel. Rebellion is often very subtle and difficult to see in ourselves at first. The Heart is deceptive and the Adamic Nature is quick to self justify. We must be objective with our lives and use the enlightened eyes of our Heart (Ephesians 1: 18) to discern darkness from light, Flesh from Spirit, and evil from good.

This is the only way to tell the difference between good and evil. Rebellion comes in many degrees, but it is all rebellion. When the pressure of the Wilderness is upon us, we may find ways to cope with it which are outside of God's provision for us. Our provision is only in Him. He is the only One who will satisfy. It is difficult to respond correctly. In fact, the men and women who have in the past travelled this road are the ones Scripture describes a being "men of whom the world was not worthy" (Heb. 11:38). If the battle to overcome the Flesh doesn't cost us everything, then it's not over. It is a battle because the Flesh does not give up without a fight. When in the Wilderness or other stage of the Process, we may find ourselves doing things we have not "given into" since we were first saved. These failures, in themselves, are not particularly important, except that they may reveal what is going on in the Heart. More importantly they are symptoms, or leaves on a spiritual tree, but not the root cause. By seeking God, we can see what is the root of our actions. In this stage of the Process, what usually surfaces is the Heart reaction that God doesn't really love us or He wouldn't let us suffer in need. This is the Flesh reacting to God's sentence of death for it; however, we will never overcome the Flesh, except by the power of the Holy Spirit. We can't work harder and be better Christians. That is carnal Christianity, and the work of the Flesh. It is not by power or might but only by the Holy Spirit that we will become what God intends for us. When we work at overcoming our outward weakness (symptoms), it only covers up the deeper root areas God is attempting to expose in our Heart. We may be able to lop off a branch or two of the tree but the tree is still standing. When the Holy Spirit does His work, He lays the axe to the root of the problem.

The root issue God addresses in the Wilderness is unbelief which manifests as fear, anxiety, striving, stress, tension, irritability, sleeplessness, worry, etc .... We may be aware of what is going on within us, or we may not. But if this stress and tension continues to build, they will eventually boil over into some kind of coping behaviour. Some of us will go on a shopping spree, have too much wine at dinner, eat a box of chocolates or two, or try and cope by "vegging out" in front of the TV. Whatever the method of coping, they are symptoms of a rising level of fear. The more God puts us in circumstances which expose our unbelief, the more extreme our coping behaviour will become. Rather than becoming self condemning for these actions, we must see this as our cue to seek the Lord for a revelation of what is alive in our Heart that the Father wants to take to the cross. The Holy Spirit is the only way into freedom for the situation, and the rebellion or coping behaviour is only a symptom of what the Holy Spirit is putting His finger on. When we turn to rebellion or coping behaviour, whatever it may be, we postpone the confrontation with the Flesh that the Holy Spirit has prepared. In the Wilderness, when our behaviour becomes quite unchristian like and we recognize the symptoms, it means God is prepared to put his enemies to flight. The situations God chooses for us are always just what we don't want. They are situations in which we have no grace. They make us confront our fears head on. The Wilderness journey is a journey of exposing all of our worst fears. Job said that the thing that he feared, came upon him (Job 3:25). If we fear, we are not in faith and therefore not able to be protected from it by God. He wants to expose and redeem these fears which are buried in our Heart and which are a part of the Flesh Nature. God's purpose is to expose through circumstances the things we can't do by grace (faith). Everything that happens to us happens for a reason. These circumstances are designed specifically for us, to expose and redeem all our weaknesses. The Wilderness is a place of fear of failure and weakness. We may appear foolish, or pathetic in the situation and be prompted by well meaning but ignorant Christians to rise up and take charge of the situation. Like Isaac, who was surrendered to his father on the altar, our lives are to be "living sacrifices". When we appear to have failed in the eyes of those who have no understanding, we must believe that no matter what, God is faithful to His promise. If we follow Him in surrender day by day, He will bring us to the Promised Land. He is the only one who knows the way because each of us has a different path. If we take up our life, we will lose it, but if we fully surrender our life even in a dry and weary place, we will be resurrected new in Christ with Him.

I sought the LORD, and he answered me; he delivered me from all my fears. Psalms 34:4 NIV

The Wilderness is not only a dry and weary place of need, it may turn out to be the greatest place of revelation and discovery of God in our entire lifetime. Usually, the Process prepares us for our ministry by refining our character, but also by revealing truths, wisdom, and understanding which will become the "cornerstone" of our ministry. It is not uncommon that throughout this period of the Process we will receive revelation which will be lifelong motivational truths which contribute to our perspective and make us an unique and valuable gift to the Church. What we learn in the Wilderness will tell us a lot about who we are, including what we specifically are called to do in the Kingdom and how we may do it.

God hardened Pharaoh's Heart in order to send the plagues upon the Egyptians to reveal His favour and power to the Children of Israel. He performed a series of miracles which none of the Egyptian sorcerers could match. Yet He said that the works that He would do in the Wilderness with His people, Israel, would be much greater. They would be greater because He was going to directly involve Israel in the supernatural provision and deliverance. He would personalize their walk with Him. When they left Egypt, God told them to write down all the miracles that He had done for them to remind them of His loving kindness towards them. Moses was instructed to keep an account of all that had transpired between God and His people, and that from generation to generation they were to recount His deeds.

There are two purposes for this. First, this would provide understanding of God and His ways for a people who would later experience their own personal Wilderness. Secondly, these accounts of God's miraculous deliverance and love would encourage the faith of those who themselves were being tested in the Wilderness. One of the greatest weapons of warfare is the accounts of our fellow heirs who have also walked through the desert with a loving, powerful, and awesome God. If others lasted through this same Process, and left for us an account, we ought to make frequent use of this for our encouragement and understanding. Jesus wants to give encouragement (faith) in a dark moment and understanding, so we will not sin in the Wilderness against the One who loves us.

Power Of Choice

In the Wilderness, the power of our choice will literally determine our destiny. We will make our choices based on faith and knowledge of the loving kindness of the Lord, or we will be part of an unbelieving generation which will rebel against God and His preparation in our lives. We must understand His purposes and His ways and continue to believe He is the one who will reward those who diligently seek Him. If we sin, we have an advocate who will quickly come to our defence so that we can recover from our folly and move on. Our greatest pitfall is to judge God in our Heart and thereby bring the Process to a halt. It is not something we can always see, since our Heart is spirit and only the Holy Spirit can open a window for us into the spirit realm. It is wise for us to regularly check our relationship with God. As David put it: "*Seek and know me, and see if there be any wicked way in me.*" (Psalms 139:23-24) He understood that a Heart can turn from God in a moment and bring to a halt all that He is doing.

So as the Holy Spirit says: "Today, if you hear his voice, do not harden your hearts as you did in the rebellion, during the time of testing in the desert, where your fathers tested and tried me and for forty years saw what I did. That is why I was angry with that generation, and I said, 'Their hearts are always going astray, and they have not known my ways.' Hebrews 3:7-10 NIV

God took Israel into the Wilderness, in part, to humble them. I once thought of humbling as the occasional spiritual spanking God gave us when we got out of line. I have since come to see humbling in an entirely different light. I see the beauty of being of humble circumstances or position. Jesus' whole ministry was characterized by this attitude. He could have "wowed" the most prominent people of Israel but He didn't. Humility is also the character of the Holy Spirit. He will always lead us into a place of weakness, poverty and humility because that is His very nature. If we embrace humility, we have put on one of the greatest battle garments available to any Christian. In our weakness, God becomes our defence. We will find intimacy with Jesus in our lowest of moments because that is where He will be found. He is with the lowly, empty, and oppressed. As painful to the Flesh as lowliness is, it is the most beautiful state to be in because that is where Jesus can truly be found. As Believers, we are called to humility so we will be like Him. We will either choose humility or we will be taught humility by God's humbling circumstances. Humility is one of the "pearls of great price" of the Kingdom which is worth selling everything for in order to acquire it. Our embracing humility and welcoming lowliness and poverty is pivotal in our acquisition of the Kingdom of God. It is in humility we gain intimacy with Christ. It is in our humility we gain grace which saves us from every enemy of the Kingdom. Jesus had all the power of the universe behind Him. He understood that it was not by power or by might, but by the Holy Spirit (Zec. 4:6). The Holy Spirit is manifest in His fullness in our lives only when we choose to humble ourselves. If grace and truth are to come to this world through the Church, it will come because we have chosen humility as Jesus did. We may think we have the right as heirs of a Kingdom to live as

Kings, but this will not change the world. Preparation for our ministry will include learning the beauty of humility just as God taught all the mighty men of Israel. We too, must also be taught it.

Experiences In The Wilderness

Although the Wilderness is a seemingly endless place of need and dryness, it does have the occasional oasis. The Children of Israel camped by one which had twelve springs and twenty-five date trees. The twelve springs were intended for the twelve tribes, so each one would have their own provision. For us, the oasis that Israel came to in the Wilderness, is Jesus. He will allow us to find Him from time to time in the Wilderness. The rock, which poured forth life-giving water for them after three days of thirst, is also an example of Christ giving us life just when we think we can't go on. Our prayer life is the foundation of our relationship with Jesus and although it may be difficult to draw near to God when we feel alone, it is important to push through. In the Wilderness we will feel we are just going through the motions of life. Only on occasion will we taste the sweet living waters of fellowship with Jesus. In the Wilderness we may wonder, "*what is wrong*?" "*What has happened?* We used to be zealous for God, now we hardly feel a thing and when we do, it is months apart. Condemnation, guilt, and fear can develop and become a further burden. We once used to enjoy revelation and the presence of God with little or no effort. Now we feel like our spiritual feet are lead and the heavens are brass.

David experienced separation from God in his personal wilderness. One character trait that pleased God was that he never forgot that God was good. Never did He accuse God with his mouth or his Heart of having anything but love for him. Many of the Psalms start out with him moaning about his circumstances to the Lord, but then he would begin to speak out faith and trust in God. He had lost His "spiritual eyes" but regained them when he sought the Lord. David took his problems to the Lord. He was renewed with fresh vision and faith that it was God who had him in these circumstances and it was God he could trust to deliver him out of them. This is the quality of a mighty warrior in the Spirit and a prerequisite for the remaining two stages of the Process. God was able to do mighty works through David because when the "chips were down", he would start out in distress and end up in praise. This was warfare because it proclaimed his choice to believe and trust God to all the heavens. He proclaimed that He was agreeing with Him and putting down his unbelief. His proclamation of the goodness of God had the power to change circumstances. Praise and proclamation also change us. They get down into our spirit and water our soul. In the Wilderness, exuberant praise and worship seem impossible most of the time, but even the simplest proclamation will refresh our soul. We must, however, continue to believe and proclaim the goodness of God. It will be a cup of cool water in a dry place.

Weapons Of Our Warfare

The Wilderness is a battle ground and when we are in the thick of the battle, every inch of ground we take further strengthens us. We must learn how to strengthen our spiritual muscles and overcome the Flesh and its repulsion for God. Speaking in a prayer language (tongue) is a helpful and encouraging practice. The effects may not be felt immediately but when they are coupled with meditating on the Lord, there are both immediate benefits and benefits over the following few days. It is a way of doing both battle and ministering to ourselves.

If our church has a prayer time at the end of the service, we should get as much prayer as we can. God will do things at a Sunday morning "altar" that may not be available at any other time. If we have people we know really love us, we should let them pray for us every week. If they don't understand what God is doing in us, then we should abstain from receiving prayer there. In the Wilderness, we are very vulnerable, and it is wise to be careful about being exposed to those who don't understand what God is doing in us. It is difficult dealing with those who have no understanding or compassion for what the Lord is doing. We must avoid these situations at all cost. They will only serve to drive us further into the desert and into isolation, which only make the journey more difficult. The best way to get regular and personal prayer is to develop a prayer partnership with another person who will pray for us, and we for them on a daily basis. A person like this can be a tremendous help to us as we move through the stages of the Process, and we can do the same for them.

Confession

Most of what we have discussed in this section outlines our defensive tools. Confession is one of our most powerful offensive tools. Acknowledging the truth to God about ourselves or about Him is powerful. When we agree with the truth, then we are able to move forward in our walk with Him. The Process is about entering new truth, and it starts with confession. In order to agree with a particular truth, it requires us to humble ourselves. When we humble ourselves, we receive grace from God and He comes and gives us the gift of repentance. We cannot repent of anything. We only "turn" from our wicked ways when God comes and transforms our Heart. He gives us a revelation of the folly and destructiveness of our sin, and when we see it, we become like God in the matter, which is to no longer be tempted by it. When we are no longer tempted to indulge in the sin, it has no power over us and we are free to "turn" from it, which is true repentance. Confession is the start of the process, and humility is the other key agent in the process. When we strive toward defeating our sin by our own efforts, God will wait until we are completely defeated and have a humble Heart before He comes. He lets us "stew" in our helplessness and inability to change ourselves until we realize we have no power within us to overcome sin. Then we can truly be saved from it, by grace, through Him;

humbling, but true. We cannot defeat sin in the power of the Flesh. Jesus said, "*can a house divided against itself stand?*" (Matt. 12:25)

Confess your faults one to another, and pray one for another, that ye may be healed,.... James 5:16

James 5:16 describes how we should use the tool of confession to both align ourselves with truth and to humble ourselves. We are to confess our faults to one another (humble ourselves) and pray for one another (confess the truth), so that we may be healed. We should embrace the opportunity to humble ourselves. It is the doorway to both healing and the treasures of the Kingdom which are righteousness, peace, and joy in the Holy Spirit (Romans 14:17). The Holy Spirit has been sent to us as our comforter. He has been sent as our teacher. It is through humility we have access to Him. It is the Holy Spirit who will give comfort and understanding of what God is doing. He delights in revealing what the Father is doing, and it is His job to comfort God's people in their time of trouble. We may call on the Holy Spirit for comfort and understanding. He is a friend and a constant companion for those who will walk with Him in humility and surrender.

Fasting

Whenever we cannot see with the eyes of our Heart what the next step is in the journey, it is good to set aside a few days to fast and pray. The very nature of fasting subdues the Flesh and puts it under the authority of the Spirit. It strengthens our will and underscores our choice to make the Holy Spirit Lord. When we fast, it is vital to let someone close to us know that we are seeking God and to have them pray for us during that time. This increases the result of fasting. It is important to fix the amount of time and the nature of the fast before starting. It is very easy to compromise on the length or the method of the fast when we are in it. A compromise in this area is a minor form of defeat. The time during the fast is usually a slow uncomfortable death. I have found that some of the best revelations come at what I call the "golden hour", which is shortly after breaking the fast. Using fasting to get understanding, or revelation or as a regular way of "putting the Flesh in its place" is helpful in our walk and a discipline which will bear fruit for the Kingdom.

Denouncing

Our words have power, and as powerful as it is to proclaim the truth, it is also powerful to denounce the power and authority of a particular sin in our life. Once we can see what sin the Holy Spirit is exposing, we should ask the Lord for forgiveness and denounce it. I am particularly careful about superstitions, but I have noticed that if a sin is denounced three times it seems to have a greater effect. I have found some Scriptures that support this, but I only recommend it for your personal observations. I say, if it works, do it, especially if it frees you from sin.

The tools of our trade as living sacrifices of the King of Kings, are: confession/repentance, fasting, and denouncing. We are a people who are called of God to be the warriors of the Kingdom and who will not only be wearing the full armor of God, but will also have the sword of the Spirit in our hands. We will declare the authority of our God over the nations and destroy the works of the Devil. The first step in the journey is to overcome the Flesh. The Lord has provided for us a full arsenal which, under the guidance of the Holy Spirit, will defeat all the enemies of God and His Kingdom. God is training an army of warriors who will overcome and bring glory to Him.

What Happened In The Wilderness

The events of Israel's journey from Egypt to the possession of the Promised Land were constructed by God for their good and our instruction. Much of the Old Testament runs parallel to the New Covenant. We can see Jesus between the lines in many of the accounts of the Children of Israel. Jesus is revealed in the process that Israel went through to be fully set aside for God. It also reveals the steps in the Process which we must pass through when being prepared for ministry. The following is an analysis of the events of Israel's journey from bondage to blessing which reveal God's steps in the process of sanctification.

Plagues And Plunder

The story begins eighty years before God's deliverance of Israel. First, He prepared a man through whom He would lead Israel out of Egypt. For the first forty years of his life, Moses was educated in the court of Pharaoh. The second forty years, he was educated and prepared in the courts of the King of Kings. On the exterior, Moses' time in the wilderness herding sheep for Jethro was quite unimpressive; however, the value of that time is not fully appreciated until Moses is well into his call. God very miraculously confirmed Moses' commission as leader of Israel. The first event occurred when Moses threw down his staff and it became a snake which consumed the other snakes produced by the sorcerers of Egypt. After that, Moses went on to bring ten other plagues which were far greater than the Egyptian sorcerers could overcome. Moses became highly esteemed to Israel and in Egypt. This was not something that tempted Moses' Heart. He was considered by God to be the meekest man on the face of the earth at the time. Meekness is not weakness, it is knowing who God is. It puts a person in right relationship with Him as Lord and them as servant. It is this understanding at an experiential and Heart level which is the prerequisite for fruitful ministry. It is our walking with God as Moses did in His personal Wilderness that we learn humility and surrender which are necessary for God to flow through us, and to trust us with His power.

Israel was told to request from the Egyptians their gold and silver and clothing which became their plunder of the people of Egypt. God demonstrated to Israel that He was powerful, that He was their God, and that He could do anything to provide for them. They received the plunder by grace, which is important for us to recognize. For us, this could be compared to a prophetic word. It was the first instalment of His abundant provision for Israel. It gave them something to hang on to in the Wilderness when they could not see where they were going. God often begins our journey with a prophetic word of Scripture which we must cling to when the times get tough. He may also confirm the word with some form of supernatural provision or blessing to seal the promise in our Hearts, as He did with Israel.

Israel spent 430 years in Egypt, **to the day**. Everything was controlled by God, down to the finest detail. This proves that all that happened to Israel happened for a reason, and it revealed God to Egypt, to Israel, and to us as Lord of all things. Our journey will be just as precise and timely. Everything that happens to us, happens for a reason. We are completely in His capable hands when we set out for the Promised Land. We do not know where we are going and we do not know when we will arrive, but nothing will happen to us that God hasn't ordained, and we will arrive on time. This is the comfort we have as we spend months and years wandering and wondering when God will resurrect and deliver us. We can be sure that His motive is love and his timing is impeccable. We will arrive on the very day He has appointed.

The Cloud And Pillar Of Fire

By day and by night the presence and guidance of the Lord was with Israel. A pillar of fire must have been dramatic. Israel needed a constant reminder that God was with them. They were not filled with the Holy Spirit who witnesses to our spirits of His presence. Israel learned to become submissive to the manifestation of God. They stayed when the cloud and fire stayed, and moved when the cloud and fire moved. The cloud and fire represent the Holy Spirit in our lives. We are baptized in water and in the Holy Spirit, and in fire. We must learn submission to His Lordship and to His authority to lead us. We must recognize His constant presence with us and not grieve Him by rebelling. This is an early stage lesson for the Spirit-filled Christian. It is one of the most important lessons to learn since so much depends on our being obedient to the Holy Spirit. God will test us on our obedience and teach and train us to discern His voice from others and from our own.

The Red Sea

The Red Sea experience was the first real test of faith that the Lord put Israel through. It was a do-or-die situation. The very powerful and impressive armies of Egypt were bearing down on Israel and they were also confronted by the Red Sea. It was God who told them to camp there. The sea looked like part of their destruction but it became their escape and their method of deliverance. Israel did not see God as their deliverer. When the situation became threatening, they were not able to trust Him. In spite of the miracles of the ten plagues, Israel was unsure of God's motives. The armies of Egypt had been their oppressors. They had reason to fear them. In the early part of following the Holy Spirit in the Wilderness, God will lead us out of our bondage which oppresses us. He will also demonstrate to us His power and faithful ability to deliver us and meet our needs in any situation. We can and should trust Him. Israel didn't trust God at this point and He was very understanding of their unbelief. After Egypt's armies were destroyed, Scripture says that Israel feared God. They recognized His power and authority and believed Him and Moses. The more that God does for us, the more He proves Himself to us as our loving and able Father. We must remember His faithfulness when He puts us in "do or die" situations and search our Hearts for unbelief. Each level of His deliverance is a new level of believing in God's love for us. It stretches our faith to trust in God's faithfulness when we are in a situation where we can depend only on Him.

The Wilderness Of Shur, Bitter Waters Of Marah

Israel had no water for three days which is about the limit for survival. They were desperate and when they got to Marah, the water was bitter. In the natural, anyone would have been wondering *"where is God?"*. Every detail of this journey was appointed for a purpose. It may have been in Israel's mind that if God could do the miracles of Egypt and the Red Sea, "*why would He let them suffer like this*"? *"Does God enjoy watching them in pain*"? They did not understand His purpose or His ways so they could not see that He was exposing their Heart attitudes through this circumstance. The bitter waters represent bitterness in our life. Bitterness can manifest in many ways, but one expression in particular that characterizes bitterness is the "glass is half empty instead of half full" attitude. Bitterness makes us see only what we don't have. We cannot be thankful for what we do have. The debtor who owed a million dollars was forgiven, but could not forgive the person who owed him fifty dollars. Bitterness distorts our view of life because we feel cheated. We have no regard for our blessings, only our losses. The bitter Heart only sees the glass half empty, not half full. It made Israel want to prove that God really didn't love them. How could God let them suffer, if He loved them? They couldn't see or believe that this was necessary in order for them to get to the Promised Land.

Bitterness is seen in our tainted actions as a response to our previous wounds. Life makes everyone bitter, because it is impossible to avoid hurt. Only Jesus can make the bitterness of life sweet, yet so many of us never let Him heal us. Bitterness causes us to blame others for our pain. Bitterness usually causes an over reaction to circumstances which threaten us with loss. We may react "strongly" when eyes of faith should rejoice in gratefulness. The Flesh will justify this reaction with self-justification and denial. The world is wrong in our Hearts and we are right. We cannot see the circumstances objectively; we see them through our anger over our perceived losses.

If we cut ourselves and do not receive treatment for the wound, it will become infected. The infection makes the cut more painful. Any normal contact with the area will cause pain. In order to bring healing to the wound, it must be cleansed and that usually causes pain. Jesus is the branch that was thrown in the waters of Marah to make them sweet. He is our antiseptic for the bitterness of our Heart. We must forgive those who have wounded us as a first step in the process of healing. As long as there is pain in our Heart, there is usually unforgiveness. The value of a clear conscience toward God is that we will no longer react to Him and others out of bitterness. The Children of Israel could not see God as good as soon as He did not meet their needs the way they expected Him to. The real test of their faith was how they would react when He seemingly wasn't there for them. We MUST NOT judge God as being against us. This is a prerequisite for going on to the next stage of the Process. Our relationship with Him cannot have any potential for breakdown if we are to go into battle against our enemies. If we don't believe He loves us when things get difficult then we can never defeat our enemies. The exposing and healing of our Heart is His mercy toward us, even though the process is painful. He will let us suffer in order to bring us to healing. He looks at our "highest good", not just the immediate situation. When we realize the love, joy and peace that God is attempting to bring us into, it is well worth the suffering. This has been called, "a severe mercy". For Israel and for us, the exposing and healing of bitterness is painful, but the victory is well worth the cost.

At the Waters of Marah, God made a promise to Israel that if they would not walk in the ways of the heathen nations who were in bitterness, that He would heal/keep them from all disease (Exodus 15:24-26). That promise is also made to us if we allow God to cleanse our Heart. Every promise has a condition attached to it and the Process of healing of bitterness may take many visits to the Waters of Marah. The healing of bitterness toward others and God is one of the most important works of redemption in the Wilderness because it makes us thankful to Him for even the painful things of life. It puts to death the mistrust and rebellion we have toward God, and allows us to fully surrender to Him because the sting of the painfulness of life has been healed. God will complete the task of exposing our Heart of bitterness if we will respond in repentance and faith toward Him. If we are suffering under a disease or other chronic spiritual or physical condition, it may be connected to bitterness toward God or others. When bitterness is the cause of a disease, we are unable to respond to God in faith for our healing. First, we must deal with any unforgiveness toward others or God, then we must ask for healing from the pain of the wound. Revelation by the Holy Spirit is required to see the condition of the Heart, but God honours our simple prayer calling out to Him even when we don't have revelation. If we know we are in bitterness because it has been exposed by our reactions, we should turn our attention to our own healing rather than let the Flesh blame others for our pain. When we respond to our hurt in the Spirit, and not in the Flesh, we can enter the blessing for which God brought us to the Waters of Marah. If we respond to God in faith, trusting that in spite of the painful circumstance of the situation, there is a reason He has brought us here. If we accept the spiritual view of the circumstances and respond to Him in it, there is treasure of the Kingdom waiting for us.

Elim Oasis

Israel moved to the next "station", which was an oasis with twelve springs and seventy date palms. The experience at Marah was draining and God provided a place for them to rest and be refreshed. The oasis which Israel named "Elim" was relief from the dry place from where they had come. They probably wished that they could stay near to the water and dates until they entered the Land of Milk and Honey. They had no strength for war or the battles that were to come. The Renewal which has swept the world in the last few years has been, for those of us who have been a part of it, an "Elim". It has been refreshing and reassuring to us who have been wandering in the Wilderness that we are on the right track. In spite of the difficulty of the journey, it has been confirmation that God is with us, and is fully in control of our lives. It is at these times of refreshing that we may feel that we are now ready to enter the promises of God. We feel we are full of power and authority and wonderful things are about to happen but it is only the beginning of the preparation.

The Wilderness Of Zin
He humbled you, causing you to hunger and then feeding you with manna, which neither you nor your fathers had known, to teach you that man does not live on bread alone but on every word that comes from the mouth of the LORD.
Deut. 8:3 NIV

It was in the Wilderness of Zin that God began feeding Israel with manna. They were fed every day. They could not store it up. They learned to live day-to-day. They were completely dependent on God to feed them. There was nothing extra, only enough to exist. They were out in the middle of nowhere with nothing to do, and with no apparent reason for being there. They had a purpose but they were not really moving forward in it in their eyes. In our life with God in the Wilderness, He will deliver us from the love of the world. There is a season in God when we will feel like we are pathetic in the eyes of the world. We, too are out in the middle of nowhere, seemingly doing nothing and just surviving. Our Flesh wants to have purpose and meaning and productivity and justification for our situation. It is difficult to explain to others why we are where we are, because without spiritual eyes and understanding, it is foolishness to them. Even to us, it may appear that the Lord has chosen to consume our life as a burnt offering to Him. Even if we never accomplish a thing, never enter the promises as Abraham did, or ever see fruitful ministry, it is enough to have been obedient to God. That is the best attitude we can take in this step of the Process. The Wilderness becomes a place where there is nothing on the horizon. There appears to be no future, no hope, nothing but an existence. It puts to death our ambition and our need to "do" in order to be justified before men. We also learn to fully trust God for every one of our needs. It puts to death our control of our life. The righteous man will live by faith, the Scripture says (Heb. 10:38). Our faith in God will be our supply. It is the love and promise of God to us that is our source, not the circumstances of the natural. God would not let Israel build up a reserve of manna. Reserves are for the fearful who do not know the ability of their God to meet every need just at the right time. This stage is a walking forward with God and learning to face every car repair and unexpected bill knowing that He knows exactly what we need. The fear of the unknown can be a powerful force which will prevent us from walking in the Spirit. God wants to strip us of all our dependencies and make us dependent only on Him. He will never fail us. Fear may cause us to rebel and take back our life from the Lordship of Jesus and try to squirm out of the Wilderness circumstances. If we succeed in this, we may never learn the freedom of depending on God completely to meet our needs in every situation. It is fear which robs us of our health and our mental and emotional peace.

Israel grumbled against Moses and the situation. But it was not Moses that had them there, it was God. They were grumbling against God. The Adamic Nature is very deceptive. Our religiousness and our fear of God keeps us from acknowledging our rebellion and hostility toward Him. Some people have a difficult time being honest with themselves and with God, but He knows everything anyway. We are only deceiving ourselves. When we are honest with ourselves and face the way we are feeling, we are able then to repent and turn toward God instead of turning away from Him. It is to be expected that the Adamic Nature will rise up against God when the Holy Spirit is leading it to the cross. It is not us that sins but it is the sin within us. It is sin who is our enemy, not God. He only wants us to expose what is hidden in our Heart. Peace is our umpire. When we have inner peace, it is an indication that we are in the Spirit. When we are in unrest in our spirit, we are usually in the Flesh. Peace, therefore, is like a baseball umpire who calls the balls and strikes. It helps us to know what is Spirit and what is Flesh. When we lose our peace, we can assume that the Flesh is alive in the circumstance. Whenever we lose our peace and start to squirm in our circumstance, we need to ask God to show us what is at work in us, then quickly bring it to the cross, so we can return to peace.

Meribah

The Children of Israel left the Wilderness of Zin (sometimes translated: Wilderness of Sin) and went in stages to Rephidirm. They were three days without water and they complained angrily against Moses and against the Lord. Three days without water left them close to death. They challenged God this time with "*is the Lord with us or not?*". God provided water out of the Rock. The Rock, of course, is Jesus. He is our provider and our life. We know this as a fundamental of the Spirit-filled Christian life. But until our life depends on His provision, we know it as only a theory. Job knew about God but after his personal experience, he said, He KNEW God (Job 42:5).

It was at Meribah that Amalek, a descendant of Esau came out and attacked Israel. Joshua was appointed leader of the army and Moses acted as Israel's intercessor. Moses stood on the mountain overlooking the battle and raised his hands before God. As long as He kept his hands raised, they were victorious, but when he lowered his hands, they began to lose ground. This is symbolic of our surrender to God, who then takes up the battle for us. This was the first battle Israel had engaged in and it was won through proclaiming God's faithfulness and power. Joshua was a warrior by character, while Moses knew God and had favour with Him. Together they were able to bring victory and move forward in their journey. This is a good example of Israel demonstrating the pattern of interdependent and unique giftedness of the Body of Christ. The incident with Moses' father-in-law Jethro, further underscores the importance of giftedness in the Church.

Jethro And The Church In The Wilderness

Jethro "just happened" to drop by for a visit with Moses. He saw that Moses was burdened by the responsibility of judging the disputes between the people of Israel. He suggested a system which would provide better service for the people and relieve Moses. Jethro was acting as a prophet-administrator because He saw the problem and was able to provide the answer that God had for the situation. Moses was very close to God, but God did not tell him directly. There were other "great" men of faith in the camp, like Joshua and Caleb, but He used Jethro to bring to Him the word of the Lord for the problem. This is a clear demonstration of giftedness in the Church and the way God intended us to respect and honour the grace that is on each life. The men who were appointed to judge Israel were appointed based on their giftedness and wisdom which is a further illustration of the "grace" in the Church.

The Wilderness Of Sinai

Three months to the day after Israel left Egypt, they entered the Wilderness of Sinai. God left us this testimony so we would know that the Process is not random. It was here that God gave The Children of Israel the Ten Commandments: religious law, economic law, and social and hygiene law. The law of quarantine and hygiene that God instituted for Israel would protect them against things they did not understand. They would be protected against disease and germs, even though they didn't understand these concepts. All they had to do was obey the laws. It took almost 5000 years before these truths were "discovered" by 20th century society. Only in the past 150 years have these principles been implemented widely in our society. The arrogance of the Flesh wants to understand something first. It wants to "do it, itself", at a huge cost of human pain and suffering. It is not God who is responsible for the pain of this world. He has provided an escape if we will only obey. If Israel obeyed, they would not suffer the consequences that other people did, even if they didn't understand why they were doing something. If God was going to redeem a people and save them, He would have to teach them to obey and trust Him. Many of the things He wanted to do with them and for them, they would not understand. Yet without full obedience, they would suffer the consequence of their rebellion. God's punishment was to keep them from going further into disobedience which would have brought even further consequences. When God corrects, it is not out of anger but love for His people.

One of the most significant laws included the procedure for dealing with sin. Harsh as it may seem, many of the sins were punishable by death. For us, this death means being cut off from our source of life - God. John talks about sin unto death, and sin not unto death (1 John 5:16-17). Old Testament law required a period of purification of 24 hours, other sins are unto death. They require confession to God and take three days and three nights to be restored to complete fellowship with Him (according to the Old Testament pattern). There are consequences for sin in spite of forgiveness available in Jesus. We are warned not to take His blood (forgiveness) for granted.

The law required Israel not to depict God with images of silver or gold. He was bigger than their wildest imagination. While Moses was away on the mountain for 40 days, the people prevailed upon Aaron to mould a golden calf. He did not have the strength of character to withstand their demands. The Adamic Nature hates authority. Aaron did not have the relationship Moses had with God and did not have the authority to control them. The rebellion which had been previously in their Hearts had now become open rebellion. Without the authority of Moses and the Law which He was bringing, they had the potential to get out of control and do evil. The Law was given for the purpose of restraining those who have no authority in their life. When we are given the Holy Spirit, He is the summation of the Law written on our Hearts because if we follow Him, we will not fulfill the lusts of the Flesh. When Aaron was questioned about the calf, his excuse was revealing. He blamed Moses, saying that he should have known that these were a rebellious people, prone to evil. He said that they pressured him and that when he threw the gold into the fire out came the calf. The golden calf is the expression of the Adamic Nature which wants tangible evidence of God. How many people claim that they would serve God, if they could only see Him, or if He proved Himself in a tangible way to them? God will not be controlled. He will not manifest Himself the way we want Him to. He will not accommodate our Flesh. We must meet Him on His terms and not expect Him to accommodate our fleshly desires. The Flesh is His enemy and He is a consuming fire which will burn up our rebellion, self-reliance, unbelief, independence, and pride.

Moulding the Golden Calf was a point at which God had had enough of Israel's rebellion. They would not obey or trust Him. He decided that He would not be tried by their evil any longer. He would no longer walk with them, but would send an angel. Moses interceded on behalf of the people just as Jesus does for us throughout this Process. We cannot go into the Wilderness without sinning and trying God. But, we have an intercessor who is much greater than Moses.

And he passed in front of Moses, proclaiming, "The LORD, the LORD, the compassionate and gracious God, slow to anger, abounding in love and faithfulness, maintaining love to thousands, and forgiving wickedness, rebellion and sin. Exodus 34:6 NIV

The Promise

Then the LORD said: "I am making a covenant with you. Before all your people I will do wonders never before done in any nation in all the world. The people you live among will see how awesome is the work that I, the LORD, will do for you. Exodus 34:10 NIV

God promised to do even greater things than He had done in the past with Israel. The plagues, water from the Rock, and the Red Sea would not compare with what He was going to do. He was referring to the defeat of the nations of Canaan. The miracles of Egypt and the Red Sea may seem like "greater things". God, however, was speaking of what He was going to do in us. To change a man's Heart took the blood of His Son and a work of sanctification that was far more wonderful and miraculous than parting the Sea or producing water out of a rock. The transformation of the Believer's Heart from being ruled by the Flesh to being surrendered and ruled by the Holy Spirit is far greater than physical miracles. It is the completion of the promise to Abraham that God would set apart for Himself a people who loved Him with all of their Heart, mind, and soul. God would deliver them and make them a people unlike any other people on the face of the earth. He would empower them and share His authority with them because He could trust them with it. These people would be the redeemed New Adam.

The Ark Of The Covenant

The Ark of the Covenant is our assurance that God will dwell with us. We are the temple of the Holy Spirit. Another parallel to the Church can be drawn here as well. When Israel was making the Ark, God filled certain people with understanding, wisdom, and knowledge by the Holy Spirit. Proverbs says that these are the three things necessary to establish a house (Prov. 24:3-4). God also provided nine different abilities (craftmanships) which were required to build the Ark. These can be likened to the nine manifestations of the Holy Spirit, which are for the building up of the Body of Christ. God has left us a witness of the things He would do and how He would do them in the New Covenant Body of Christ.

Blessing Of Obedience

He will bring you to the land that belonged to your fathers, and you will take possession of it. He will make you more prosperous and numerous than your fathers. The LORD your God will circumcise your hearts and the hearts of your descendants, so that you may love him with all your heart and with all your soul, and live. The LORD your God will put all these curses on your enemies who hate and persecute you. You will again obey the LORD and follow all his commands I am giving you today. Then the LORD your God will make you most prosperous in all the work of your hands and in the fruit of your womb, the young of your livestock and the crops of your land. The LORD will again delight in you and make you prosperous, just as he delighted in your fathers, if you obey the LORD your God and keep his commands and decrees that are written in this Book of the Law and turn to the LORD your God with all your heart and with all your soul. Deut. 30:5-10 NIV

The promises made to Israel have been taught by the Church as simple formulas for temporal prosperity; however, they are not only the commands to Israel but were meant to be prophetic words for the Church today. Circumcision was the Old Testament way of being set aside wholly for God. The circumcision of the Heart is to put to death the Adamic Nature and to walk in obedience to the Holy Spirit. The prosperity spoken of in this Old Testament Scripture is a prosperity of abundance for us found in the Kingdom of God. Love, joy and peace in the Holy Spirit is by far more precious than the wealth of this world. This is what the Kingdom of God is about. Prosperity is to see the work of your hands bear fruit for the Kingdom and to lay up treasure in Heaven. To have fellowship and an intimate relationship with the Father will produce more satisfaction and peace than anything available in this world. To know peace which no situation can dethrone is a blessing worth more than a lottery fortune. In most cases, people desire wealth in order to satisfy every want they can conceive. Unbridled consumption will never satisfy. In Christ, we have provision for every need, and death to every fleshly desire which would only take us away from loving and serving Him.

Disobedience

The consequences of disobedience are fear, sickness, discontent, striving, unfruitfulness, and lack of purpose. These are, for the most part, conditions of the Heart which manifest in the natural. The final consequence of disobedience will bring a sword against us which symbolizes destruction. To become a slave of obsession or illness or immorality is to be victimized by the lusts of the Flesh. It will consume our body, our mind, and our soul with fears. It will consume our life with the folly of fruitless pursuits which is destruction. God warned us of disobedience and gave Israel and us a clear view of the result of our choices. If we want to live a fruitful content life, free of the lusts which drive others down dead-end streets, and after things which cannot satisfy, we must allow the Holy Spirit to put the Flesh in us to death. There can be no compromise with the Flesh.

The Wilderness Of Paran

The Wilderness of Paran could be called the "wilderness of rebellion". Until now, Moses was able to minimize the impact of Israel's unbelief by using his "influence" with the Lord. In Paran, Israel went into open rebellion and challenged Moses and the Lord's authority. It was here that Israel said "*it was better to be in the bondage of Egypt than to be in the Wilderness with God.*" (Num.11:1-18). To Israel, their situation seemed unbearable. They wanted meat to satisfy their lust and even Moses was "fed up" with them. God in His wisdom gave them not just enough, but so much that they were repulsed by the meat they had wanted.

It did not satisfy them even though they had more than enough. God will prepare us to deal with an area of the Flesh by allowing us to rebel and try to satisfy ourselves. There is a season in the Process when God gives us the things that we think we want just to show us that there is nothing satisfying in them. When we eventually see our folly and confess our sin to God, we are free of the power of the Flesh in this area. We hate what we thought we would love and turn back to Him for help. There is a window of opportunity here to be free. When we see our sin and do NOT confess it to God, we have effectively made our choice and given the Flesh power over us, instead of crucifying it. The pleasure, if we could call it that, returns to our Fleshly activity and He gives us over to it. We become deceived by our lust and become enslaved to our Flesh in this area. If we don't confess our sin to God when we have a chance, we can become worse off than when we started. The opportunity to be free is available to us only for a short time. Our lack of a response is a response, therefore we must take the opportunity to be free when it is presented. It may be a long time until the Spirit will again provide this same opportunity. If we respond to God in confession and agree with our revelation of the truth, we will be free. If we postpone it, we will miss the opportunity.

Miriam And Korah

Both Miriam and Korah rebelled against the Lord and challenged Moses' authority. Miram was humbled and Korah was destroyed. The difficulties of the Wilderness exposed the deeper levels of unbelief that were in Israel's Heart. They had been in the Wilderness a long time and nothing seemed to be happening. It isn't hard to be deceived by the Flesh. Nothing that God was doing seemed to make sense. In the natural, Miriam believed that she could do it better. *"It couldn't be that difficult to find the Promised Land and go into it."* They rose up in their own understanding (the Flesh) and took charge of the situation. They rationalized their rebellion by insisting that Moses was incompetent. What a mess they would have made of God's plan to redeem them. If they had succeeded, they would have compromised, used logic and temporal understanding and made treaties with the inhabitants of the land. Israel would have become just like the nations of Canaan and not the redeemed people of God. The Promised Land would have been nothing like the promise that was made to them. This is a pitfall that can happen easily to us. Israel leaned to their own understanding and rejected the leading of the Holy Spirit because it did not make sense to them. The things of the Holy Spirit are foolishness to the natural understanding. If we rebel, God tries to bring us back to obedience to the Holy Spirit. In the Wilderness, Korah and his men were destroyed. God does not "pluck us up" to purify the Church as He did in the Wilderness of Paran with those who rebelled. In mercy He tries to bring us back on track through His discipline. Sometimes it comes in the form of illness or other circumstances that are meant to cause us to evaluate our ways and seek Him. Even the most spiritual Christian will rebel in the Wilderness. Rebellion is in our Hearts. We were born into it. We may be very "spiritual" and believe we are beyond the folly of rebellion, but then circumstances bring up from our Heart feelings and attitudes we never imagined we had. When we do rebel, we must find our way back to the Lord by seeking for the root cause of our rebellion. Usually it is our unbelief in the love of God. In difficult circumstances the Adamic Nature accuses God of not loving us. This is unbelief in God's true nature. It could be called believing a lie about God. Once we accept the lie as truth, it is a simple progression to: "*I can do it better on my own*". This enthrones the Adamic Nature and it is the reasoning of the carnal Heart. It will lead to rebel against the Lord, and send us on futile pursuits and aimless wandering in the desert.

The Spies

The spies who were sent into the Land of Canaan brought back an exaggerated report of the strength of Canaan, but it exposed Israel's Heart of unbelief. Caleb and Joshua spoke faith to them, but they would not repent. God was not so affronted with their fears as He was with their rebellion and stubbornness which prevented them from repenting. He was aware of their Heart but His plan was circumvented by their refusal to repent. Israel had been captive in Egypt. They had a slave mentality. They didn't believe that they could be the conquerors of such a choice land. Many Christians are called today to conquer certain "nations" but they don't feel competent to do something so grand in their own eyes. The story of the talents told by Jesus in Matt. 25 is the story of Israel in this stage of the Wilderness. Their fears and the past were influencing their perception of the future. They were afraid they would fail, so they shut everything down rather than risk defeat. They were looking at the situation with the natural eyes instead of with eyes of faith in God's ability to make them victorious. They did not know their Father and they did not know His commitment to their success.

God does expect us to doubt from time to time, because He knows our Heart. He wants us to have our faith renewed in Him. David allowed the Holy Spirit to rise up in Him and open his eyes of faith. God can do mighty works through His people when they allow Him to build their faith. God must be our closest friend. He is the One we must go to when we lose our peace. No matter how terrible the situation, David handed His troubles over to God. We cannot please God without faith. All of our good works are for nothing if they are not done in faith. David completed the course God chose for his life. He was fruitful in His day and His life was inspiration for millions of Believers who came after him.

Death Of A Generation

In one sense, the death of a generation is symbolic of God putting to death our Old Man and resurrecting a new spiritual man who is surrendered to the Holy Spirit. In another sense, this part of the story is a warning to Believers that if we do not deal brutally with our unbelief, we will never enter God's promises of love, joy, and peace, prosperity and rest, and the fulfilment of our call in fruitfulness. These promises are for those who are obedient not to the Law, but to the Holy Spirit.

In the fall of 1988, I asked God why He was doing what He was doing in me at that time. Usually I do not get such an immediate or clear response. What rose up from my Heart were these words: "*After I was baptised in the Holy Spirit, I immediately went into the Wilderness*". Simultaneous to these words reaching my mind, I saw with the eyes of my Heart that the Church had experienced the latter rain of the Holy Spirit spoken of in Joel 2:28. More people had been baptised in the Holy Spirit in the last 50 years than in the last thousand years. The Holy Spirit was falling on the Church.

"And afterwards, I will pour out my Spirit on all people. Your sons and daughters will prophesy, your old men will dream dreams, your young men will see visions. Even on my servants, both men and women, I will pour out my Spirit in those days. Joel 2:28 NIV

It began at Azusa Street in 1906 and seemed to wane about 1980. There had been the Pentecostal Movement, the Jesus Movement and the Charismatic Movement. Many of those people had entered into the things of the Holy Spirit and then were called into the Wilderness. I could see how many of them were "shipwrecked" in the desert. They had run aground on materialism, unbelief, rebellion, stubbornness, and other pursuits of folly. They were a dying generation.

The farmer sows the word. Some people are like seed along the path, where the word is sown. As soon as they hear it, Satan comes and takes away the word that was sown in them. Others, like seed sown on rocky places, hear the word and at once receive it with joy. But since they have no root, they last only a short time. When trouble or persecution comes because of the word, they quickly fall away. Still others, like seed sown among thorns, hear the word; but the worries of this life, the deceitfulness of wealth and the desires for other things come in and choke the word, making it unfruitful. Mark 4:14-19 NIV

Our personal Wilderness is designed to expose the unbelief of our Hearts. Usually that is painful. It may seem that God does not love us if He will let us suffer. He only comes when we are at the end of ourselves. He comes and delivers us when we become broken, defeated, and despairing of life itself. It is then that we are ready to receive. It is then that the beauty of humility and complete surrender to Him begets the grace that saves us.

We must not "stumble" in pursuing the "word of our calling". If we get hung up in the circumstances, discouraged or rebellious and stubborn, the "word of promise" may never be fulfilled. The parable of the sower and the seed applies to the Church who is seeking the fullness of the Kingdom of God in its life. If our unbelieving Hearts overcome us and we agree with the lies, then we are defeated. Without a firm root of faith and trust in God, we cannot stay fixed on what He has for us, but instead we look for immediate gratification or the path of least resistance. It may seem too hard to allow God to purge our Hearts. But we do not have a choice. We must be fruitful, or be cut off (John 15:5-6). The rewards of a fruitful life are well worth temporary discomfort. If we lose our life, we will find it. That is the real life. The full rich life. The prosperous life. The happy fulfilling life. We are trading in emptiness, futility, the cares of this world and the deceitfulness of riches which do not satisfy; we are trading in the raging lusts of the Heart that pull us in directions which only waste our time and energies for the Abundant Life. If we love this world, we cannot see the Kingdom of God. If we become entangled in its systems, it will consume our life, and destroy our Heart of faith and calling. The defeat of Jericho and the Seven Nations are too great for us. Only the blood of Jesus and the power of the Holy Spirit can overcome them. We must be faithful and enduring to the end.

The pitfalls are many, but the faithfulness of our God is great. Mercy and grace are our best friends and the intercession of Jesus will sustain us even in our most rebellious times. Everything that happens to us happens for a reason. The Flesh sees this as foolishness, but the Spirit is leading those who will be led into paths of righteousness. He loves us and is always waiting for the prodigal son to return to Him. God is not threatened by our rebellion against Him. He is not afraid to let us go off on our own path. He knows we have nowhere to go. Everything else is futile and unsatisfying especially after we have known the satisfying goodness and provision of God. "*Man does not live by bread alone.*" (Luke 4:4) We must re-dedicate ourselves daily to allow Him to test us and humble us and redeem our Hearts, so we can be the pure and spotless Bride, when our lover, Jesus, returns for us.

Chapter Seven

Stage Two: Jericho

"I have seen these people," the LORD said to Moses, "and they are a stiff-necked people." Exodus 32:9 NIV

The Wilderness is a dry and weary place that seems to go on and on forever. It tests a man over time to see if he will believe God. Abraham believed God even though time was not on his side, and God counted it as righteousness (Romans 4:3). When the Children of Israel crossed over the Jordan, they were in the Promised Land but they did not possess it. In the Promised Land, the manna ended and Israel ate of the produce of the Land. This was a confirmation to them of their victory in the Wilderness. It was also encouragement that they would possess the Land, even though there were many nations still to depose.

Jericho became Israel's biggest obstacle. As an army, they were virtually unarmed compared to the nations of Canaan. Jericho had walls which in the natural were insurmountable. However, Israel was a generation of faith and they had had some victories to encourage them. When the spies visited the city, Rahab believed that they would be victorious in spite of the walls. Her faith saved her and her entire family. For six days Israel marched around Jericho, not speaking a word as the Lord had commanded them. During the time they marched, they focused on how God would deliver them. He was building their faith as they faced their enemies. At Jericho, the objective changed. The Children of Israel believed God and were obedient. They did their fighting against their enemies instead of attacking God. This was a significant change in Israel's relationship with Him. They recognised their enemies and trusted God for victory.

The Jericho Walls

The walls of Jericho were not only thick but also very high. The people who built the city were anticipating the worst. They had fortified themselves in what they perceived to be a safe place from a very hostile environment. Some of the nations that Israel would face came out against them. Their defence was an offense, but Jericho was different. Their main defence was the walls. In Scripture, cities are often interpreted as the Heart of man. The walls of the city were its defence. In the case of the heathen nations, the Lord revealed that these walls were protection that unredeemed persons use to protect themselves. They are walls that God wants to tear down. These walls don't protect. They become a prison for us and they stand between our Heart and God. These walls of idolatry prevent God from completely reigning. They represent the things that captivate our Heart that are not the Lord. Sometimes we occupy our time instead of using it wisely, especially when it comes to doing spiritual things. Our mind is filled with a hundred urgent matters when it should be quiet before the Lord. We often accuse the Devil of causing this, but it is not always the Devil, it is primarily the Flesh. Anything which is more important to us than God is idolatry; the unredeemed Heart is full of idolatry, which is spiritual adultery. In stage two of the Process, God deals with those things which entice us and keep us from loving Him with all our Heart.

Jesus replied: "A certain man was preparing a great banquet and invited many guests. At the time of the banquet he sent his servant to tell those who had been invited, `Come, for everything is now ready.' "But they all alike began to make excuses. The first said, `I have just bought a field, and I must go and see it. Please excuse me.' "Another said, `I have just bought five yoke of oxen, and I'm on my way to try them out. Please excuse me.' "Still another said, `I have just got married, so I can't come.' "The servant came back and reported this to his master.

Then the owner of the house became angry and ordered his servant, `Go out quickly into the streets and alleys of the town and bring in the poor, the crippled, the blind and the lame.' "`Sir,' the servant said, `what you ordered has been done, but there is still room.' "Then the master told his servant, `Go out to the roads and country lanes and make them come in, so that my house will be full. I tell you, not one of those men who were invited will get a taste of my banquet.'" Luke 14:16-24 NIV

The Kingdom of God is illustrated by Jesus as a wedding feast in which the invitees have other more important things to do. They all respectfully decline the invitation of the Host. Obviously they are known to Him, since they were on his "A" invitation list. All of the reasons that were given in themselves were with some merit, but they should not have taken priority over the invitation to a friend's wedding. The guests' wrong priorities kept them from the invitation. Idolatry is characterized by improper priorities in our life. The Flesh will mercilessly invade and disrupt our efforts to have a time alone with God. The Flesh fills our mind with trivial concerns when we want to pray. Our worship is shortened by our wandering mind when we are enjoying the sweetness of His presence. The walls (idolatry) of the Heart must be put under the authority of the Holy Spirit. He wants to make us free to be obedient to Him. He wants our priorities to be His priorities. He wants to free us of the pursuit of temporal things which bind us to this earth and keep us distracted from the things of eternal value.

Jericho is unlike the Wilderness in that it is an intense and extreme battle and much more of a definitive death than the slow agonizing death of the Wilderness. Without the work of redemption done at Jericho and at Ai, we cannot go on to defeat the Seven Nations. God called Israel rebellious and stubborn. This was not only their problem. He also accused Saul of rebellion and idolatry and because of it took the Kingdom from him (1 Samuel 15:23). If we, as a people of

God are to be true revolutionaries in this world, we cannot have any love for the things of it. We cannot surrender. We cannot make peace. We cannot compromise with the idolatry of the Heart. We must totally destroy it as Joshua did to Jericho and Ai.

The LORD your God will drive out those nations before you, little by little. You will not be allowed to eliminate them all at once, or the wild animals will multiply around you. But the LORD your God will deliver them over to you, throwing them into great ***confusion*** *until they are destroyed. He will give their kings into your hand, and you will wipe out their names from under heaven. No-one will be able to stand up against you; you will destroy them. The images of their gods you are to burn in the fire. Do not covet the silver and gold on them, and do not take it for yourselves, or you will be ensnared by it for it is detestable to the LORD your God. Do not bring a detestable thing into your house or you, like it, will be set apart for destruction. Utterly abhor and detest it, for it is set apart for destruction.* Deut. 7:22-26 NIV

In the Wilderness, God dealt with Israel's unbelief (rebellion), and at Jericho He dealt with Israel's idolatry. One of the manifestations of idolatry is (spiritual) stubbornness. We are not obedient to God when we are in idolatry because we have other objectives. Most of us have been beckoned by the Spirit of God to come away and fellowship with Him but we were watching our favourite TV show. We cannot be lead by God when we are in idolatry. Idolatry makes us act stubbornly toward the Lord. In its simplest form, it is easy to detect but idolatry is more subtle than this. We can presume we know what God wants and think we are acting for Him when we have not heard or been lead by the Holy Spirit. This was the sin that the Pharisees fell into and it is also idolatry. Religious teaching controlled by an idolatrous Heart interprets Scripture without the revelation of the Spirit. We act stubbornly before the Lord because we assume we know; therefore, we take charge. This is the work of the Flesh and not the Spirit. It is common to man, but almost impossible to see in ourselves. Only the "eyes" of the Holy Spirit can discern our Heart.

Idolatry Of The Heart

For rebellion is as the sin of witchcraft, and stubbornness is as iniquity and idolatry. I Sam. 15:23

Another manifestation of idolatry is anything that we may use to create an image of ourselves. When we are separated from God by our sin, we do not know who we really are. The Adamic Nature does not want to surrender to God so it attempts to provide distractions (lusts of the Flesh) which will take us away from the Lord. These lusts are compelling and become idols in our lives without us consciously giving ourselves to them. They are an abomination to the Lord because they occupy His place in our life. We don't openly worship these things, but when they take God's place in our life, it is the same as worship. All of these things are vanity. They are designed to create an identity outside of Christ. For this reason, God has not been able to speak His destiny and Lordship into these areas of our Heart. These are the pursuit of things that make us feel we are valuable in the sight of others. They are vanity and foolishness that we give ourselves to instead of the Lord. We must strive and toil to achieve even the smallest level of fulfilment from them and even then, they don't last. Only the Lord can fulfill us, and when He speaks love and destiny to our Heart, it brings us to rest from our striving for fulfilment. The Promised Land is the place of rest and abundant provision. When God tears down the walls of our Heart which stand between Him and us, and speaks life into us, we are fulfilled and cease from our striving. We are not aware of the striving and vain pursuits to which we give our energies. When life is over, much of what we have spent ourselves on will have no eternal value. There will be no businesses, cars, fancy houses and retirement savings plans. What a waste of a life for which Jesus died. These "vanities" of the Flesh begin in the Heart but are conceived in the imagination. It is there where the battle is fought.

Vain Imaginations

Casting down imaginations, and every high thing that exalteth itself against the knowledge of God, and bringing into captivity every thought to the obedience of Christ; 2 Cor. 10:5

The unredeemed Heart is subject to passions and lusts which "promise" to bring pleasure. They are conceived in the mind as imaginations, or visions, which the Heart offers as ways to bring pleasure, fulfilment and to bolster the identity. They happen so frequently during the day that they go almost unnoticed for what they are. These imaginations, however, have the potential to captivate the mind and the Believer, if the Flesh is not crucified. These imaginations which originate out of the Heart of Flesh, are usually images of what life could be **if**........ They appear as fantasies of fulfilment, but they are really attempts by the Flesh to lead us to find fulfilment outside of intimate fellowship with God. Television is a prime example of vanity and images. It has bred an epidemic of discontent, greed and striving in our society. The pictures we see are designed to stir up the Flesh and make it respond to the images. They offer the Flesh a vision of success or fulfilment. Most advertising is manipulation of the Flesh to get us to buy a product. We are presented with images which are lies built upon lies. They cannot fulfill what they promise and what they promise cannot fulfill. These vain imaginations, if undetected, captivate the mind and drive the Believer down dead-end streets in pursuits of images of success, wealth, and significance. Fantasies of grandeur, romance, family, home and children can also be idolatry if we are striving to get these things in the power of our own Flesh.

Do not wear yourself out to get rich; have the wisdom to show restraint. Cast but a glance at riches, and they are gone, for they will surely sprout wings and fly off to the sky like an eagle. Proverbs 23:4-5 NIV

It is not only riches that captivate men's minds. The idolatry of these vain imaginations is rooted in not knowing who we are in Christ. When we first come to Christ, we cannot understand the depth and implications of belonging completely to Him. We cannot fathom His unconditional love and that nothing can separate us from Him. The "fallen" Heart will not accept these concepts. The idea of being saved and accepted just because we exist is about as foreign to us as a life without time, or God without a beginning. We do not know Him; therefore, we cannot know who we are, since our identity is in Him. Without knowing and being at rest with who we are in Christ, our Heart searches for an identity in temporal things. This identity may be our giftedness, our intelligence, our sense of humour, our preaching ability, our leadership, our wealth, our good reputation, our knowledge or our business acumen. It is anything we believe can justify us before others and give us respect. Our society is having an identity crisis. Television subtly conveys a message that discounts any identity but those which would drive us to consume. We are children of God. Our identity is intrinsically rooted in the promise that nothing shall separate us from His love. We must have a transforming encounter through the work of the Holy Spirit, which will free us from the Flesh and root our identity in Christ. This is a huge death to die, to give up the thing we have hung our identity on for most of our lives. God will create circumstances over and over again, that will pull down every bit of respectability we ever had. He will make us weak before people, and resurrect the Spirit Man which has no reputation to defend. As painful as this process is, it is one of the most freeing, because it brings the Heart to peace and obedience. We become free to cease from our striving to be something that we think will make us respectable before people or acceptable before God. This kind of idolatry is subtle and easily rationalized, but if we seek the Kingdom and righteousness, He will pinpoint and destroy the idolatry that is part of our Adamic Nature.

In the beginning of our walk with God, we have carnal desires and imaginations. As we walk with God, we trade our carnal goals and objectives for religious carnal goals and objectives. Ministry in the modern Evangelic Church is structured to appeal to the idolatrous Heart. It offers power, and authority, respect, honour and even adulation. Ministry can provide wealth, fame, and independence. Some of the media ministries throughout North America are blatant expressions of the idolatry of the Heart, and not pure and fruitful ministry. They are like ravenous wolves who devour the sheep, rather than feed them. They preach the word but it is a Gospel which leaves room for their idolatry and impure motives. They don't do it intentionally or knowingly; they have been deceived by their own Heart. There are exceptions, but idolatry is rampant in the Church.

Much ministry is motivated by ambition. Many ministries overwork and grossly underpay their employees. They show little respect or love for these servants and fellow heirs to the Kingdom of God. How can they love the lost or the Body of Christ if they can't love their own co-workers? The world is more respectful and honouring of its people than the Church. This is a common experience among those who have had ministry "experience". They have been used, abused, and cheated, all in the name of ministry. The motive of this kind of ministry is not love. It is the pursuit of the vanity of fleshly imaginations. It is ambition. Why is bigger better? Why does preaching have to be an entertaining performance? Does it make it clearer, deeper or more spiritual? Why is Hollywood style glitter a part of the Church at all? It is because the preachers and the "receivers" are attracted by the "place" this type of ministry gives to the Flesh. It feeds the Flesh and not the Spirit. This is not the character or nature of Jesus or the Holy Spirit. God is misrepresented not by the words spoken, but by the spirit in which the Gospel is presented. He is also misrepresented by what is **not** being preached. It is another Gospel.

If that is how God clothes the grass of the field, which is here today and tomorrow is thrown into the fire, will he not much more clothe you, O you of little faith? So do not worry, saying, 'What shall we eat?' or 'What shall we drink?' or 'What shall we wear?' For the pagans run after all these things, and your heavenly Father knows that you need them. But seek first his kingdom and his righteousness, and all these things will be given to you as well. Therefore do not worry about tomorrow, for tomorrow will worry about itself. Each day has enough trouble of its own. Matt. 6:30-34

Another expression of idolatry in our lives is setting goals. Nowhere in the New Testament is there instruction to set goals. We are instructed to live day-to-day without giving a thought for tomorrow. The Flesh rises up against this. It ratationalizes that we or the Church cannot operate like this. But how do we know what the Lord will do, or provide for us in the future (James 4:13-17)? It is folly and idolatry to set goals unless the Lord reveals them to us in order to pray them into being. It only leads to striving, unrest, idolatry and evil as the Lord Himself calls it. God rarely gives us goals because He knows how weak we are in the Flesh. We will run ahead and do things our own way and mess it all up. He has a tendency to give us only enough information for us to move forward today. He does not give us orders and then let us "run with it". Living day-to-day requires a new level of dependence, trust, and submission to the Holy Spirit. This leaves no room for the Flesh. We cannot march to the sound of our own drum. When we are impatient and anxious and over focused on accomplishing a certain mark, rather than "being", it is a sign that the Flesh is alive in us. This is the way of the world, not the Kingdom. If we cannot sit in God's presence in peace because we feel we must be doing something, accomplishing and self-justifying, we are being tortured by the Flesh. In the Kingdom, it is out of "being", that we do. In the world, we *do* in order to *be*. The world and the Flesh says, "*you have to prove yourself and earn your way*". It is not so in the Kingdom of God. We have been justified by faith and given the Holy Spirit in whom is our inheritance as Children of God. As we surrender to Him, we acquire the Kingdom and its treasures. Everything we need in this life, and the next, is in Jesus Christ. The Holy Spirit has been given to us to lead us into His provision for every area of our life. He will never leave room for the Flesh.

Choose Poverty

In today's world, poverty (modest means) is considered to be a sign of failure, but in the Kingdom of Heaven it is a role of honour (James 2:5). Paul said that he knew how to be content in abundance and in need. He became poor in material things in order to become rich in spiritual things and to minister them to the Church (2 Cor. 6:10). There is even a greater benefit to choosing poverty than for the sake of fruitful ministry. It is in poverty that intimacy with Jesus can be found. It was the poor with whom He spent his time. It was the weak He nurtured and healed. It is in the emptying of every power of self that we arrive where Jesus can be found. He chose to become poor, so we could become rich (2 Cor. 8:9). He is there in intimacy when we choose to be like Him. Poverty (weakness) is freedom, not bondage, as the world would portray. Wealth has with it the burden of protecting our assets against loss, and piloting our own ship into an unknown harbour. But in poverty, we have the promise of God's provision, which is more trustworthy than a fat bank account. When we choose poverty we put to death our fleshly desire for financial independence and self indulgence. We are saying by our choice that we will depend upon the Lord for our supply and not our own efforts. We are setting our life goal to be the pursuit of the treasure of the

Kingdom, rather than temporal things. For those who haven't experienced intimate fellowship with Christ, there is nothing else but to amass temporal wealth. Unfortunately for them it is folly. When we give up the pursuit of material things in life and pursue the Kingdom of God, we gain one of the greatest treasures available in this world - intimacy with Christ. The Flesh ceases to strive when the Holy Spirit nails the lust for control over our own circumstances and the deceit of riches to the cross. We may appear to be failures if we choose poverty, but the value to us is freedom, powerful fruitful ministry, and a beautiful fellowship with Jesus.

Stumbling Blocks

From that time on Jesus began to explain to his disciples that he must go to Jerusalem and suffer many things at the hands of the elders, chief priests and teachers of the law, and that he must be killed and on the third day be raised to life. Peter took him aside and began to rebuke him. "Never, Lord" he said. "This shall never happen to you" Jesus turned and said to Peter, "Get behind me, Satan! You are a stumbling-block to me; you do not have in mind the things of God, but the things of men." Matt. 16:21-23 NIV

It is the Flesh that has taken the suffering out of the Gospel. It is the only way to the treasure of the Kingdom. The Flesh is a stumbling block to the things of the Spirit, and the things of the Spirit are a stumbling block for the Flesh.

Jews demand miraculous signs and Greeks look for wisdom, but we preach Christ crucified: a stumbling-block to Jews and foolishness to Gentiles, but to those whom God has called, both Jews and Greeks, Christ the power of God and the wisdom of God. For the foolishness of God is wiser than man's wisdom, and the weakness of God is stronger than man's strength. Brothers, think of what you were when you were called. Not many of you were wise by human standards, not many were influential; not many were of noble birth. But God chose the foolish things of the world to shame the wise, God chose the weak things of the world to shame the strong. He chose the lowly things of this world and the despised things—and the things that are not—to nullify the things that are, so that no-one may boast before him. 1 Corinthians 1:22-29 NIV

The weak and the despised are chosen by God, but to someone in the Flesh, this is a stumbling block. Weakness is despised in this world. Vulnerability is hated. For those in the Flesh, they look for signs of success as indications of right standing. They cannot "read" the things of the Spirit, which are lowly and despised by men. The most Godly of men in the Bible had no credentials other than the call and affirmation of the Holy Spirit. To the humble, these men were seen with spiritual eyes for their gifting, call, and ministry. It was the Pharisees who were offended by their lack of human (Flesh) acceptability. They were abhorred by these men's lack of regard for the Flesh's gatekeepers. The values of the Flesh are not the values of the Spirit and therefore truth is often presented in such a way as to be a stumbling block to the arrogant. Jesus said that the Kingdom of God is hidden to those who are not humble (Mark 10:15). When the things of the Spirit are measured by the Flesh, they will always appear to be foolishness. The things the Spirit of God will lead us to do will be a stumbling block to Christians who are carnal and unable to read the purposes of God. They see and judge the works of the Spirit by the Flesh, using Scripture and carnal understanding to judge the Spirit. Therefore, there are two Gospels and two Churches, and they are together. There is the carnal Church and there is the Spirit Church. These Scriptures about the Kingdom of God confirm a two Church Kingdom.

Not every one that saith unto me, Lord, Lord, shall enter into the kingdom of heaven; but he that doeth the will of my Father which is in heaven. Many will say to me in that

day, Lord, Lord, have we not prophesied in thy name? And in thy name have cast out devils? And in thy name done many wonderful works? And then will I profess unto them, I never knew you: depart from me, ye that work iniquity. Matt. 7:21-23

"I am the vine; you are the branches. If a man remains in me and I in him, he will bear much fruit; apart from me you can do nothing. If anyone does not remain in me, he is like a branch that is thrown away and withers; such branches are picked up, thrown into the fire and burned. John 15:5-6 NIV

This is an account not of the world, but of the Kingdom of Heaven. It is an account of Believers who are judged as unbelievers because they did not walk in the Spirit. They lived the Scriptures but didn't surrender to the One who wrote them. The Scripture is a stumbling block to them. It is idolatry that stands between them and their Saviour. These are the walls of Jericho. People like this run their own lives, based on their interpretation of the Scripture, but they have a carnal understanding. They live life to satisfy the Flesh, pursuing things that will never satisfy. Paul was conscious of the subtle difference between walking surrendered to Christ and independence and idolatry. Even after all he suffered and accomplished, he warned his fellow workers and himself to not get overly confident because that would beget independence (1 Cor. 9:26). It is only by humbling ourselves and giving up our lives, that we will find the treasure of the Kingdom. We can please God only one way. It is to walk in faith, trusting Him with all areas of our lives, by surrendering them to His Holy Spirit. All else is dead works, which are the works of the Adamic Nature.

Idolatry comes in many forms and there is not a Christian who is not subject to it. The key to discerning what is Spirit and what is Flesh is that the Spirit always brings victory in humility, peace and sweet fellowship with Jesus. The Flesh stirs strong emotions, anxiousness, and a wall of separation from God that can't be bridged. It likes to pretend it knows what God would or would not do. By doing so, it sets itself up as judge of what is God and what is not. God is unpredictable. We do not know Him completely. The Pharisees never imagined that He would send the Messiah and then let Him die on a cross. Doing what we think God wants is usually more pleasing to the Flesh, than the Spirit. God will never condone the works of the Flesh by joining us in intimate fellowship if we have chosen "our way". He rewards us with Himself when we choose death to the Flesh. The pleasure of the works of the Flesh is always shallow because there is no lasting fulfilment in it. But when we choose the Spirit, we also gain the presence and beauty of the Lord, and in Him we are completely fulfilled.

Identity

The Devil challenged Jesus on His identity. He said, "*if you are the Son of God*" then prove it. Jesus was secure in who He was. He had nothing to prove to anyone. He just wanted to please His Father. He did not have to prove He was the Son of God. He knew the love of the Father and who He was. He had chosen poverty, no reputation, and lowliness. He was free of the struggle to "be". He had nothing to accomplish but the will of the Father. He was free to serve Him. He had no other agenda or motive. He was the one who was being tested in the Wilderness, it was not God on trial. It was not who He was that mattered, it was who His father was that mattered most of all to Him.

Then the Devil took him to the holy city and had him stand on the highest point of the temple. "If you are the Son of God," he said, "throw yourself down. For it is written: "He will command his angels concerning you, and they will lift you up in their hands, so that you will not strike Your foot against a stone." Jesus answered him, "It is also written: 'Do not put the Lord your God to the test." Matt. 4:5-7 NIV

The root of idolatry is the lack of knowing who we are in Christ. Our identity has been established by who our parents, teachers, and friends say we are. But God sees our spirit. The essence of who we are is resident in our spirit. Our giftedness and calling, personality, and preferences are part of our being which is resident in our very core. Only by the revelation of the Holy Spirit can we see who God has created us to be. Only by a word of affection and love can we realize our enormous worth to Him. It is our worth to Him that establishes our identity. We are Children of God, redeemed and given a life in Christ that is characterized by His love for us. When we have been touched at the Heart level by His love, the walls of our Heart that protect and imprison us come down. We are free to live our lives open to God and to man, without fear. We can be who we are, and never fear that anything will change or separate us from the One who has made us one of His own. Our identity can never be shaken and the folly of "identity crutches" are seen for what they are. We are no longer seeking approval or adulation from the rest of the Church or the world. We are free to be who we are, and to follow Him regardless of what that might look like to others. Hearing "*Well done good and faithful servant*" is more important than anything else for the servant whose Heart is fully set on pleasing Him.

The Law

"*Woe to you, teachers of the law and Pharisees, you hypocrites you clean the outside of the cup and dish, but inside they are full of greed and self-indulgence.* Matt. 23:25 NIV

As good as the Law is, it is never good enough. Jesus came to provide us with what the Law could not. When He ascended, He said it was better that He go, so the Holy Spirit could come (John 14:26). It was better for us because Jesus could only be in one place at one time. He could teach only with words. The Holy Spirit blankets the whole earth. He can live inside us and teach us with spiritual revelations and visions in the "eyes" of our Heart. Jesus is our justification before God. The Holy Spirit has been given to us as our teacher, comforter, deliverer, and our friend. All that God does in our life is done by the Holy Spirit. He is our "connection" to the Father. The purpose of the process of sanctification is to enable us to more fully walk in obedience to the Holy Spirit. When we walk in the Spirit, we will not fulfil the lusts of the Flesh. That is to say that we will not do anything that is sin, or foolishness, or displeasing to God. If we walk in the Spirit, we will not be unwise, or unkind, or selfish. We will not fall prey to the deception of the enemy since the Holy Spirit will warn us, or protect us. In the Holy Spirit there is complete and total fulfilment of the intent of the Law which Jesus summed up to be: *to love God with all of your Heart soul, strength, and mind, and your neighbour as yourself* (Luke 10:27).

The unsanctified Christian will take the principles of Scripture and try to live them. He will order his life and pattern it after the Law and attempt to walk in it. The human nature loves to find the principles of Scripture and with the power of the Flesh do them. The Pharisees were the greatest at studying the Law and applied it meticulously to their lives. Yet it was they who Jesus found to be the most despicable. The Pharisees were "able". They understood the Scriptures because they studied them. They worked diligently to follow them, day and night, and it was all for nothing. The people with whom Jesus spent time with and in whom He invested His short ministry, were completely "unable". These are the humble of Heart. They were failures, losers, hopeless, and despicable in the eyes of the Pharisees because they broke the Law. The Law cannot justify, yet it is the Law and its principles we continue to teach and revere throughout the New Testament Church. We don't openly call these the Law; the Flesh is never that blatant. We teach "principles", and the Flesh loves principles. It rises up with principles in its hand, and attempts by will and determination to live in them, falsely promising that this will please God. The Law was not good enough to justify us before God because it qualifies the "able", and disqualifies the "unable". Principles are for the "able". They are for those who still have enough confidence in the Flesh to attempt to live "up" to the Law. But God's plan was just the opposite. He intended to save the hopelessly "unable". The observance of the Law only puffs up and further crowns the Flesh Lord. Principles become stumbling blocks to following the Holy Spirit. The Pharisees thought they knew all about God, but they missed Him when He came. The Law or the observance of laws and principles is idolatry in the sight of God. It keeps us from surrendering to the Holy Spirit and following Him into sanctification. Our Flesh wants to lean to our own understanding of Spiritual things. We have made a place for the Flesh in the Church by hiding from God behind His Law. We have built walls around the observance of principles instead of surrendering to His Spirit with sayings that are neither true nor Scriptural. For example, it is commonly said that, *"the Holy Spirit will never lead you to break God's Law"*. The implication of this is to say, *"Just follow the Law; it is the same as the Holy Spirit anyway"*. Yet Jesus, under the leading of the Holy Spirit, broke the Law on several occasions. When the adulterous woman was brought to Him, He was obliged to condemn her to death by stoning, which is what the Law required, but He didn't. He neither turned her over to her accusers for punishment or accused her Himself. He did this by the direction of the Holy Spirit. He broke the Law. She should have been stoned or at least reprimanded for her sin. Jesus fulfilled the Law by providing us a way to love God with all of our Heart, mind and strength. We are to fulfill the intent of the Law by walking in the Spirit. The Holy Spirit will lead some people some times to break the written Law. David ate the sho bread which was punishable by death, yet he did not perish. The Law had its purpose, and now that the Holy Spirit has come, we are not subject to the Law but to the Holy Spirit. Why is the law so prevalent in the Church? It makes a place for the Flesh. The Church has been afraid to trust the Holy Spirit in their fellow Believers. They don't believe the Scripture John 10:27, "*my sheep know my voice.*" They try to justify principles and other manifestations of the Law and the Flesh because they are afraid the Church will become lawless. They see immaturity in some of the sheep and want to protect them and the Church's image with rules rather than trusting God and teaching them how to hear and obey the Spirit. The Church is not structured to bring proper correction through mentoring, therefore it has had to compensate by making laws. This has created a hierarchical structure in the Church. Without ever saying it, members are working up a ladder toward their opportunity to be useful to God and acceptable to the Church for ministry based upon their ability to observe laws. This structure accommodates the Flesh. We are qualified by the unmerited favour (grace) of God, not by our ability to observe rules. Isn't the qualification for ministry the flow of grace? If God choses and condones by His Spirit, who are we to stand in judgement? This system is carnal and builds the ego and the self-image, and it does not please the Lord. He hates it. Doing the right thing in our eyes will never accomplish the work of the Holy Spirit. We could be knowledgeable in all the principles of the Gospel, even the things of the Holy Spirit, but if we are not walking in humility and surrender to Jesus, we are like the unbelieving generation of Israel. It is the Holy Spirit's job to put to death its enemy, the Flesh, and to resurrect the Spirit Man. It is the Holy Spirit's job to prepare us for ministry which is fruitful, and that can't be accomplished by observing the Law.

You who are trying to be justified by law have been alienated from Christ; you have fallen away from grace. Gal. 5:4

All who rely on observing the law are under a curse, for it is written: "Cursed is everyone who does not continue to do everything written in the Book of the Law." Clearly no-one is justified before God by the law, because, "The righteous will live by faith." The law is not based on faith; on the contrary, "The man who does these things will live by them." Christ redeemed us from the curse of the law by becoming a curse for us, for it is written: "Cursed is everyone who is hung on a tree." He redeemed us in order that the blessing given to Abraham might come to the Gentiles through Christ Jesus, so that by faith we might receive the promise of the Spirit. Gal. 3:10-14, NIV

Legalism subtly says that the good or bad circumstances in our life are the result of obedience or disobedience to the Word. It threatens God's judgement or blessing in a "cause and effect" Gospel. We were saved by grace and mercy because of love. We will never be able to "do it well enough" to acquire God's blessing. The new covenant is not reap and sow, but grace and mercy; how else could we be saved? As children of the New Covenant our blessings are by grace and our difficulties are our discipline and testing. Fruitful ministry is not the reward of the obedient to the "rules", but the natural outflow of having received the grace and love of God. The Law says, "be obedient, or suffer the consequences". But Jesus said that all of the Law is summed up in: "*Love the Lord God with all your Heart, soul and strength and your neighbour as yourself*" (Luke 10:27). Out of love comes obedience. We love Him because He first loved us. If we are obedient only to avoid consequences, we do not love God, we fear Him. We are not only servants, we are also sons and daughters. Sons and daughters love their Father, and because of love and trust, obey Him.

In the coming years as we approach the return of Jesus, the Church will be sanctified and cleansed of its idolatry. Lordship will be given fully to the Holy Spirit in individuals' lives and in the life of the Church. Those who refuse the sanctifying work of the Spirit and who continue to operate in the Flesh will see the true Church as heretics, because they will not observe the Law as they interpret it. The Pharisees had Jesus killed because He demonstrated power which won the people's Hearts, yet He broke the Law. The Pharisees felt they had to save God's people (the Church) from this heretic, Jesus. They "knew" He was a heretic because He did not observe "their" Law. In the days to come, there will be a battle between the Flesh and the Spirit. It will cause turmoil in the Church. The lawyers who cannot trust the Holy Spirit to guide them will fall further and further into the idolatry of their own understanding of Scripture. They will deliver up brothers as infidels. It will be the Flesh alive in the Church which will be the Spirit-filled Believer's greatest threat. There will be a dividing of the wheat from the chaff, the weeds from the grain, and the good fish from the bad fish, in the Church. It will be painful, and it will seem as though the Church cannot survive the internal war between the Flesh and the Spirit. It will be the final revealing of the true Church before the return of our Lord, just as Scripture says.

For I have come to turn "a man against his father, a daughter against her mother, a daughter-in-law against her mother-in-law—a man's enemies will be the members of his own household." Matt. 10:35 NIV

Other Laws

Those who want to make a good impression outwardly are trying to compel you to be circumcised. The only reason they do this is to avoid being persecuted for the cross of Christ. Not even those who are circumcised obey the law, yet they want you to be circumcised that they may boast about your flesh. May I never boast except in the cross of our Lord Jesus Christ, through which the world has been crucified to me, and I to the world. Neither circumcision nor uncircumcision means anything; what counts is a new creation. Gal. 6:12-15 NIV

In every family their are certain priorities, perceptions, sayings, and opinions. Some of these are good, some are evil. They usually are the expressions of the grace or lack of grace which is in a family. In my family for example, it was commonly said: "*If you want it done right, you will have to do it yourself.*" This is only one example, but there are many, many rules that are part of our prideful way of determining how one should live. "*Get a good secure job, and save your money.*" This is human wisdom which must not interfere with following the Lord, or it is idolatry. These are the "laws" we use to "judge" between right and wrong before we know the Lord. These spoken or unspoken laws are hindrances to our freedom in the Spirit. They are ingrained in us and pushed very deep in our being, and we do not recognise their effect on us. They are our justification. "*We work hard and save our money - we do the right thing*". God is not impressed. They cause us to judge others by a standard that is not the Lord's. They also cause us to try to get others to live according to our own idolatrous rules and laws. When we judge others by our human and personal "laws", we set ourselves up as God. We are justified by our own "right doing" and measure others by the standard by which we believe we can be measured. God doesn't care for our laws and standards of conduct. This form of idolatry is so subtle. Our Heart is so deceptive and wicked. We can't avoid doing this. It is the nature into which we were born. This type of legalism only causes strife and turmoil in a family and in the Church. God does not care about our laws and rules; He despises them. We are not to judge others by them. The Lord said to me once: "*they are doing the best that they can*". I realized that all people are doing the best they can, no matter if they meet a certain standard or not. They are making the best of what they have to work with. If they are broken and disillusioned inside, they are doing the best with what they have to work with. If they are tormented and wounded, they are doing the best they can in the state they are in. We cannot judge what others should be able to do, because we cannot see the woundedness and brokenness of their Heart. We are in no position to judge anyone since we are so desperately in need of acceptance and grace in our own fallen state. We must not make others subject to our, or any laws. We must rather throw off the oppression and judgement of these laws we have acquired, and surrender afresh to the Holy Spirit. Much of the strife between parents and teenage children could be skirted by taking a non-judgemental attitude toward young adults who are choosing to discover their own values. Even as parents we don't have the right to judge.

When we are subject to a Law or any authority which is not the Holy Spirit, it is idolatry in God's sight because these laws circumvent our full devotion and obedience to Him. We must do as God commanded Joshua when He captured the heathen nations - to utterly destroy them.

You must destroy all the peoples the LORD your God gives over to you. Do not look on them with pity and do not serve their gods, for that will be a snare to you. Deut. 7:16 NIV

"when you cross the Jordan into Canaan, drive out all the inhabitants of the land before you. Destroy all their carved images and their cast idols, and demolish all their high places. Numbers 33: 51-52 NIV

God will have no other gods before Him. It may be the Law, it may be our sayings, it may be our ambition, but they are an abomination to the Father.

Reputation

God is not like a man; He is not concerned about His reputation. Nobody has ever come to Jesus because He had a good reputation as a Saviour and Lord. They come because they are without hope on their own, and the Holy Spirit has revealed Jesus as the only answer. In most denominations, there is a hierarchy of pastors and churches based upon size and reputation. The Flesh wants to find acceptance. It fears rejection and seeks approval, even adulation. A pastor, church, or individual is not free to walk in the Spirit if they are seeking acceptance from others. The struggle for a good reputation is a work of the Flesh. With every perceived fluctuation in our standing, one way or the other, we are tormented by unrest. The Flesh cannot be satisfied, it must be put to death. Jesus and the spiritual men of the Bible were despised by most men. Only in the long view of history were their lives confirmed and redeemed. Martin Luther, although he had many subscribers to his Spirit-lead conviction that we are saved by grace and not dead works, had far more people in his time declare him a heretic. Who was he to oppose the established authority of the Church? To walk and stand for the things of the Spirit is to invite conflict, criticism, and dissension against our actions and our person. If we are not free of the struggle to be seen as "right" and "good" we will never be able take a stand for what we know is the Spirit's "walk" for our lives. Our reputation is a wall that stands between us and God and His purposes for us. It is good to have the opposition and hatred of some people. The image we present to others needs to be crucified on the Cross. We need to confess our faults to others openly, being transparent as sinners, redeemed only by grace. It is in this lowly position that we find freedom from the tyranny of the Flesh. Jesus picked the lowly and poor to spend time with because that is what He was. They were humbled in His presence, but the Pharisees were agitated. He reduced them to mere sinners who had nothing with which to make themselves better than others. They could not be justified by their good works in His holy presence. Pharisees operate in self-sufficiency and independence. They are looking for someone to elevate them to a new level of independence, honour, and sufficiency. As leaders, they had an image to maintain. What is the image that we project as the Church? The Church projects the image of being sufficient, able, together, capable. We present ourselves to the world as if we have it "together". We think that if we look good, we will attract people to Christ and His Church. This is misguided at best. It is for this reason we have not been able to attract the unable. These are the ones Jesus came to save (Luke 4:18). The poor and the weak know what they are, and are looking for an answer to their need. The more able and sufficient we appear to be, the less the unable are attracted to us as a Church. We want the able for our Church because they appeal to our Flesh.

The transformation of a Heart is not carnal. It is not with human understanding that we are saved. It is spiritual. It is the work of the Holy Spirit which draws people to Jesus. It is the Flesh that wants to look good. This is carnal thinking in spiritual matters. Unbelievers intuitively know that Christians aren't as "good" are we project, and many are outside the Church because we are not completely honest about who we are. In light of the Holiness of God, we are relatively no better than them - just forgiven. Leaders and the Church will gain respect, not loose it, by humbling themselves as the "chief of sinners", as Paul did (1 Corinthians 15:9). It will provide incentive for others to live in the truth about themselves and pull down the idolatry of a "good" reputation. If we become like Jesus, of no reputation, we will see the fresh wind of the Holy Spirt blow in our Churches, which will be the most attractive thing possible for Believers and Unbelievers alike. If we are considered by most people to be of good reputation, then we probably are not walking in the Spirit, because the Spirit always offends the carnal man. When we walk in the Spirit we will pay a price, and usually it is our reputation we pay it with. God will sacrifice our reputation in order to accomplish His goals in us and others. He will lead us to do the right thing rather than the thing that looks good. David put his reputation in the hands of God. He asked Him to redeem him and defend him. He was free to do what he knew was right before the Lord, without concern for what others would think. Our reputation is a matter that should be in God's hands. He will put it to death and resurrect our reputation in His good time.

Be merciful to me, O LORD, for I am in distress; my eyes grow weak with sorrow, my soul and my body with grief. My life is consumed by anguish and my years by groaning; my strength fails because of my affliction, and my bones grow weak. Because of all my enemies, I am the utter contempt of my neighbours; I am a dread to my friends—those who see me on the street flee from me. I am forgotten by them as though I were dead; I have become like broken pottery. For I hear the slander of many; there is terror on every side; they conspire against me and plot to take my life. But I trust in you, O LORD; I say, "You are my God." My times are in your hands; deliver me from my enemies and from those who pursue me. Let your face shine on your servant; save me in your unfailing love. Let me not be put to shame, O LORD, for I have cried out to you; but let the wicked be put to shame and lie silent in the grave. Come near and rescue me; redeem me because of my foes. You know how I am scorned, disgraced and shamed; all my enemies are before you. Scorn has broken my heart and has left me helpless; I looked for sympathy, but there was none, for comforters, but I found none. Psalms 31:9-20 NIV

Humble yourselves, therefore, under God's mighty hand, that he may lift you up in due time. 1 Peter 5:6 NIV

Who Is Our Teacher?

It is part of our church culture to have a teaching in almost every meeting. We have teachings on the radio, on television, on audio tapes in the car, and in Sunday morning, and Wednesday evening meetings. We are the most taught people on the planet. So much of our spiritual life is given to sitting in meetings being taught. One would think that it is through "knowing" that we are saved. Through "knowing" we are healed, delivered, or overcome the world and the Devil. How much more do we need to know before we engage in the real work of the Church, like healing the sick, and delivering the oppressed? If we were to spend SOME of that time in prayer, as a Church, we would learn far more from the Holy Spirit as He reveals His purposes and plans to us. The apostles were prepared for ministry not only by Jesus' teaching, but even more so by watching Him minister. Much of the teaching in the Church is out of duty and tradition. The 30 to 45 minute sermon is the highlight of the service; however, most teaching just "tickles our ears". It may sound good but it will not change us. It makes us think we are moving forward, but in fact we haven't moved an inch. We don't change anything, by JUST knowing. It is our traditions which contain us in a form that robs us of all God has for us, and that is idolatry. Part of the reason we do not change and flow with what the Spirit wants for our meetings, is that most members refuse to be flexible. They want it the way it always has been; they want it their way. They would leave the Church if there were changes, and then the budget wouldn't be met and then....and then..... Who controls the Church, the members or its Head? There will be a price to pay to free the Church of this idolatry, but it will be well worth it. It will separate the sheep from the goats. This is not a change that can be brought about by the hands of men, but only by the redeeming work of the Holy Spirit, in His time, not our own.

The Holy Spirit is named in Scripture as our teacher (John 14:26). This does not mean that He will not use people, but it does mean that He is our final authority on what we should retain and accept for our lives and what we should reject. There is a lot of teaching in the Church which is distorted or unbalanced truth. We must be wary of legalism and other forms of heresy. Only the Holy Spirit can save us from that. Paul warned that we are to be careful that we do not receive any other Gospel but the one through which we were saved (2 Corinthians 11:4). We must submit what we are taught to our teacher the Holy Spirit, for Him to confirm and to give meaning to it for our lives. It is He who will make what we learn relevant. We must depend on Him for our teaching, using whomever He chooses to be His agent. If we want to learn and grow, we must put our need for knowledge, wisdom, and understanding in the Holy Spirit's hands. The Church may well be His agent, but it is He who we must acknowledge and make our teacher. Anything else is idolatry.

Ai And The Devoted Things

Israel has sinned; they have violated my covenant, which I commanded them to keep. They have taken some of the devoted things; they have stolen, they have lied, they have put them with their own possessions. That is why the Israelites cannot stand against their enemies; they turn their backs and run because they have been made liable to destruction. I will not be with you any more unless you destroy whatever among you is devoted to destruction "Go, consecrate the people. Tell them, 'Consecrate yourselves in preparation for tomorrow for this is what the LORD, the God of Israel, says: That which is devoted is among you, O Israel. You cannot stand against your enemies until you remove it. Joshua 7:11-13 NIV

When Israel went up against the city of Ai they were soundly defeated. It should have been an easy victory, but they were beaten badly by their enemies. At Jericho, God banned Israel from taking the gold and silver as spoil. But Achan saw a beautiful silver lamp and could not resist taking it. He hid it in the ground in his tent (Joshua 7:21-22). For this reason, the Children of Israel were defeated. They had hidden things to which they were devoted. For the New Covenant Believer, the hiding of a devoted thing speaks of holding back something that should be devoted to God. The hiding of it in his tent indicates that this is a Heart issue. Achan had coveted the gold and silver of the heathen nations (the world). He was not free to be obedient because the lusts of his Heart overruled his devotion to the Lord. The things that are hidden in our Heart are the reason we are weak and lack the authority over the enemy in our lives.

Achan coveted silver and gold. Although this can mean money or wealth, it really refers to temporal things in general. The hidden desire of the Heart for the temporal comforts and pleasures of this world are like a thorny weed which will choke out the good seed (prophetic word of calling) in our life. A house divided against itself cannot succeed. With a Heart seeking after temporal love, we are vulnerable and not fully armed to take on the battles of the seven nations. We are stuck where we are and cannot go forward until we put to death by the Holy Spirit the thing that is alive in us. Achan's silver and gold were hidden. Our deepest loves get buried because the carnal nature wants to hide from God. It is our love of these things that make them so offensive to God. It is blatant idolatry and it stands between us and Him. If we covet the things of this world, we lose some of our authority as Believers, and hinder our relationship with God. We must not hide our desires from the Lord. He sees them. They are empty and vain, and leave us unfulfilled anyway.

Examples Of Idolatry

When Jesus said that, "*the love of money was the root of all evil*", He was speaking about the seeking of self rule and power that does not come from God. He was speaking about the power of money. In this world, money is power. With money you can do what you want, buy what you want, go where you want. Nothing is out of reach if you have money. You are master of your own destiny. The Flesh loves money because it empowers it. Money can feed the Flesh with power and indulgence. When God sets to put the Flesh to death, the first thing He does is remove the power of money. Disposable income, credit, and reserve cash are consumed by the fire of God. He makes us dependent on Him. It is through this we learn obedience to the Holy Spirit. He will put us in situations where we cannot do as we please. We learn to give everything into His hands when we are helpless without Him. We can only move forward if He opens the way. Things we wouldn't think of committing to prayer must now be won as Spiritual victories. We learn that everything must be covered in prayer and surrendered to the Holy Spirit. This is a painful transition. We cannot buy, do, or go where we want without the Lord providing. Eventually, we see the folly of our idolatry and appreciate what the Lord is doing in us. We see the things we did to satisfy the lusts of the Flesh and are grateful for the mercy and grace of the Lord that has put them to death. We enter a new freedom and intimacy with the Lord which we did not have before. It quiets the Heart and puts to death the raging passions and lusts of the Flesh, so we can "walk" in the Spirit.

It is hard for a rich man to enter into the Kingdom because he has power. He has no needs. He has everything he wants here on earth. The poor man, however, is disenfranchised, despised and without power to help himself. The poor are closer to the Kingdom of Heaven than the rich (Matt.19:23). When Jesus told the rich young ruler to sell everything and follow Him (Luke 18:22), He was saying, that all his good deeds were not good enough for him to enjoy the treasures of the Kingdom. Humility, which is to be helpless and know it, is the gate into the Kingdom and its treasures. As long as we are empowered with anything other than the Holy Spirit, the Flesh will use it for independence and disobedience to God. Can a man be rich and be surrendered to God? Wealth built by the arm of the Flesh is a stumbling block to our spiritual growth. Wealth, spiritual or natural, which is provided for by the Spirit is joy and peace. Only the Holy Spirit can reveal to us, which it is. Either way, the "call" is God's. He knows just how to put the Old Man to death. He will consume all our sources of independence, in just the perfect way.

The "Prosperity Gospel", as it is called, is based on Scripture but it has been distorted and is a stumbling block to the Church. We are called to die to independence and self-rule. The prosperity of the Gospel is not material things, it is a promise of the treasures of the Kingdom which cannot be bought with money. They are far more valuable than silver and gold. The Gospel is not a means to material gain, nor is it the "good life" in temporal terms. Jesus' Kingdom is not of this world, nor are love, joy, and peace and the fulfillment that comes from fruitful ministry in our calling. The great weakness of the North American Church is materialism, and it has modified the Gospel to accommodate carnal Believers' pursuit of its folly.

The Church has been compromised because it is afraid of the consequences of taking a stand. People would leave the Church or cut their giving and there would be a number of repercussions from there. The Church has become an organization rather than the Body of Christ. It is an organization which like other organizations has financial needs. It is bound by its material needs to a compromised Gospel. Pastors and leaders are held hostage by their fear of not having enough money if they did what they believed was best for the Church and its members. This is common in many Churches. Under the circumstances, "nobody is willing to rock the boat". There are other reasons for compromise, but the organization called the Church and its huge financial needs have become idolatry which keep the Body of Christ from being completely free to follow the Holy Spirit,

Then some Pharisees and teachers of the law came to Jesus from Jerusalem and asked, "Why do your disciples break the tradition of the elders? They don't wash their hands before they eat!" Jesus replied, "And why do you break the command of God for the sake of your tradition? For God said, 'Honor your father and mother' and 'Anyone who curses his father or mother must be put to death.' But you say that if a man says to his father or mother, 'Whatever help you might otherwise have received from me is a gift devoted to God,' he is not to 'honor his father' with it. Thus you nullify the word of God for the sake of your tradition. You hypocrites! Isaiah was right when he prophesied about you: "'These people honor me with their lips, but their hearts are far from me. They worship me in vain; their teachings are but rules taught by men.'" Matt. 15:1-9

The work of the Flesh has not changed since the beginning of the Church. It likes to organize, quantify and contain the Church with rules that will make it predictable and controllable. Through rules and law, the Flesh can gain control of the Church. In the Church, there has been no greater example of control and the work of the Flesh than in the teaching of tithing. If there is human control of the income of a Church then it can be organized and plans can be made. Fleshly desires and ambitions can be appeased quite easily. It is an opportunity for the Flesh. The argument that the Church needs order is nonsense considering it was the Holy Spirit who gave order to the universe. His order seems like disorder to the Flesh because it is not in control. This argument for order is a manifestation of the battle of the Flesh with the Spirit for control of the Church.

One of the great idolatries and manifestation of legalism and the Flesh in the North American Church is the prolific teaching of the practise of tithing. It is theologically unsound. It is clearly an observance of law, rules, the Law, or guidelines. They may sound good but, if it is not the Holy Spirit who is Lord over our giving, we have missed Him. Until now, the Holy Spirit has tolerated this, but now the Lord is raising up voices against this practice. Recently, a renowned Bible teacher has come out and openly declared tithing as a legalistic observance that has no place in the Spirit-filled Believer's life. Since he is so well respected, it is hard to dismiss him as a fool, or heretic. He will be criticised for his stand and may well suffer attempts to discredit him. From a scriptural point of view if we are observing "guidelines" or rules, or the Law or cultural laws, it is idolatry that keeps us from turning over full lordship of our giving to the Holy Spirit. This teaching is in fact a stumbling block to hearing the Lord clearly for what He wants to do. The teaching of tithing has been damaging to individuals but nothing like the damage it has done to the Church. Tithing has put an obligation on the Believer, and it has allowed the Church to operate like a business. Seeking the Lord for direction and guidance is a much lower priority if the income of the Church can be controlled. When we are walking in the Spirit we know that God will only supply enough for what we are to do. If we make a mistake in hearing Him, we will not have enough money to take care of the bills. It makes everyone much more dependent on God for their supply, and more importantly, it releases the power of God to supply far above the capacity of the congregation's financial ability. When we operate in the Spirit, God comes and adds, so as to confirm His Word and meet every need.

The teaching of tithing in the Church is a stumbling block to Believers walking in the Holy Spirit in their giving. If we were to make these same obligations and guidelines for worship they would be deemed by most to be ridiculous. It has become idolatry to the giver and for the Church. Giving is meant to put to death our dependence on our own abilities to get money and dependence on God for our needs. Tithing will produce a cause and effect result as part of the natural law of the universe. If you give you will receive. But God wants us to live in the blessing of the power of walking in the Spirit in our finance, so we can defeat nations and situations much greater than ourselves. When we surrender our giving to God, His promise is to meet our every need, even if it is far beyond our own capacity. Jesus demonstrated this principle in the feeding of the 5000. God multiplied what they did have, so that the need would be met. It is important for us as a Church to get to this stage of walking with God, because in the future the battles we are going to face will be far beyond what we can do, and we will need God to provide for us. Scripture says that, *"He has the cattle on a thousand hills"*. This is obviously not specifically cattle, but means that He has resources which cannot be seen. He can give favour and grace to us in any situation and through anyone in order to meet our needs. There are times in the Process that He will allow us to remain in need but that is for a specific purpose. No amount of tithing will get us out of the need which is meant to humble, discipline and instruct. The problem with the Law (tithing) is that it demands 10%, but the Spirit of God will only be satisfied with 100% (complete surrender). He will only accept complete surrender of everything, including our finances and wealth. Observing tithing as a guideline or law or suggestion or good practice is idolatry which stands between us and the Lord.

It is taught that tithing is not the Law since it was demonstrated before the Law, when Abraham tithed to Melchizedek, King of Salem (Hebrews 7:1-2). This is correct. Abraham knew nothing of the Law and without obligation or the burden of the Law, he gave a tithe to the King. He did this because the Spirit of God caused Him to do it. It is the Flesh that wants to turn what the Spirit does into some religious observance. Abraham, in obedience to the Holy Spirit, took Isaac up the mountain and was going to sacrifice him (Genesis 22:2-18). We don't try to make this into a law and have every father perform this as a ritual. There are many, many depictions of the leading of the Holy Spirit in peoples lives in the Bible, but we don't turn them into some "guideline". The Flesh wants control. It is part of its nature and the issue of money brings control to the Church over what is being done. The Church is in bondage to the Flesh in this area and needs God's victory to become free to walk obediently to the Holy Spirit. When a Church decides to follow the Spirit completely, it will be like jumping off a cliff. They will have to trust that God will catch them and He will; however, it won't be all glorious victory. There will be much criticism from those who cannot see where the Church is going and can only see the circumstances in the natural. First there is death, and only after death can there be resurrection.

Circumcision Of The Heart

Joshua took all the men of Israel and circumcised them before they entered into the Promised Land. This was a new generation who were born in the Wilderness but were not "set aside" for God. Circumcision of the Heart is the act of being set aside fully for God, not on a physical level, but on a spiritual level. The Law prescribed that circumcision be performed on the eighth day. It was not the Sabbath day (the 7th day) but the 8th day. The 8th day is the first day of the week. It was on the first day of the week that Jesus was resurrected from the dead as a symbol of the first fruit which belongs to God. The circumcision of the Heart is the destruction of the Old Man and the resurrection of the New.

When we are sanctified (circumcised in the Heart), we are resurrected on the first day of the week as "first fruits" unto God (Romans 6:4-6). We are therefore, living sacrifices unto Him (Romans 12:1). We are dead to the Law and alive to Christ. Observance of the rules of the Law (the 10% of tithing) is not enough and (100%) only complete sacrifice and surrender to the Spirit will do.

In him you were also circumcised, in the putting off of the sinful nature, not with a circumcision done by the hands of men but with the circumcision done by Christ, having been buried with him in baptism and raised with him through your faith in the power of God who raised him from the dead. Col. 2:10-11 NIV

The Concept Of A Leader

The picture of the Body of Christ in Scripture is a much different picture than that of the current Church. The Body should have a beautiful deference and respect for the gift of grace within the other members. Leaders are men and women who will make others more important than themselves (Phil. 2:3-4). They must maintain their authority and right to lead not by an authoritarian use of power, but by the respectful acknowledgement by the other members that that is their rightful, God-given role in the Body. With that role comes a responsibility, like husbands who are called to die for their wives (Ephesians 5:25). They are called to sacrifice their life for the Body as Christ did. They should do whatever it takes to create opportunity for the Body to mature and develop into fruitfulness, regardless of the cost to them. Leaders must be able to identify giftedness in others. They are the coach of the "team". Their job is to place people in the role in which they are best suited so they can be successful by grace.

Generally, the Church is carnal in the way it picks its leaders. In most cases, the elders of the Church are businessmen who can apply their skills to the financial or other logistical areas of the Church. They are people who are respected for their temporal abilities. The Church has respect for those who are powerful and who have money. Usually, they are the least qualified to lead since their methods and those of the Holy Spirit are opposite to each other. In other cases, leaders are chosen because they appear to have no needs. It would seem from outward appearance that they have their life "together". We measure spirituality by outward signs. This outward sufficiency is more of a disqualification than a qualification for leadership. Leaders must set an example of humility. It is not weakness to be needy, it is truth and humility. The real qualifications of a leader should be: can they hear and walk obediently to the Holy Spirit, do they love the Body, and are they called at this time to serve? Paul wrote to the Church that men called to leadership must be able to discern and protect the Church from false doctrine and especially the idolatry of legalism (Titus 1:9-10). One of his greatest concerns was that the "leaven" of legalism would not distort the Gospel of Grace which he taught them. Paul confronted Peter openly and quite strongly on the issue of legalism (Galatians 2:11-17). He accused Peter of going back to observing the law of the Circumcision in order to appease certain zealous legalistic Believers. Paul saw the threat of a legalistic observance of laws (the manifestation of the work of the Flesh) as a real danger to the Gospel of Grace. If we chose our leaders based upon the guidance of the Holy Spirit free from our human prejudice and understanding, we would be very astounded by whom the Spirit would choose. It would not be the Sauls. It would be the Davids.

Paul, speaking about the qualifications of leaders said: *He must hold firmly to the trustworthy message as it has been taught, so that he can encourage others by sound doctrine and refute those who oppose it. For there are many rebellious people, mere talkers and deceivers, **especially those of the circumcision group**.* Titus 1:9-10 NIV

Debates And Criticism

It is believed and taught by most Church leaders that they and the Church should not be criticized or corrected. Anyone who criticises the Church or disagrees with a leader is seen as being a troublemaker. Martin Luther was one of the more important Christians in the history of the Church. His writings reveal how he openly condemned the things that were not scriptural about the Church. Today's Church has not been very good at receiving or giving criticism. Even though it is generally considered poor "form" to criticize, it has a valid and important role in the health of the Body. Many leaders are defensive and not really open to receive sincere criticism of their ministry or decisions. It is often implied that any criticism is against God, not them, or that it is destructive, not constructive. For this reason when people see something terribly wrong, they gracefully "bow out" rather than confront the problem in love. Because of their particular gift or perspective, they are able to identify problems that others do not see. Sadly, they leave rather than confront and debate the issues and the Church is the worse for it. It is the input of other perspectives and "graces" in ministry which are safeguards for the Body's life and ministry. Inflexibility, closed mindedness, desire for control, stubbornness, and defensiveness are manifestations of the Flesh and are self and Body destructive.

The other area we as Christians avoid is constructive confrontation. Paul confronted Peter on his duplicity about not eating with the gentile Believers (Gal. 2:11-17). It is common in the Church to hear contradicting interpretation of Scripture on a variety of subjects. There is so much bad theology, even amongst sincere Believers, because most teachings are never put to the test of the scrutiny of the Body. If the teaching is given by someone renowned, it becomes widely accepted without any scrutiny. By debate, the truth is discerned and lies are exposed. Rarely, however, do we take the time to know and understand a particular theological position and determine whether it is true in the wisdom of the Spirit. Debate and criticism should be a provision in the Body for bringing the truth to the surface. It would batter a few egos but it would also make people accountable for what they say and teach. It is a work of the Flesh to try and eliminate constructive criticism and debate in order to avoid being corrected. In the **right spirit**, criticism and debate can be a positive and constructive part of the life of the Body.

The Promise Of Fruitful Ministry

Jericho is the Believer's first entrance into the Promised Land. Sometimes at this stage of the Process, God will provide a token opportunity of fruitful ministry. It is symbolic of the entrance into the Promised Land. This first release of ministry may be in the area of a Believer's calling, but it usually is a mere shadow of the main or true calling.

This "introductory" ministry may continue for a number of years, but more commonly it ends as a person progresses through the Process. At this stage of the Process, Churches have conflict, especially with those who have the prophet gifting/call. The idolatry stage of the Process will bring head-on conflicts that often cause Prophets to leave the Church. Usually at this stage, God will call the intercessors together to pray for the Church through this most difficult stage of the Process.

God uses leadership and ministry as a place to prepare leaders. Leaders who are in this Process may have been in ministry for years, but feel that they are not completely living in the full call of God. They know that their ministry is marked by areas of power and authority, but also by other areas of weakness. They may be plagued with problems which steal the joy out of ministry. "*For my yoke is easy and my burden is light*" (Matt. 11:30 NIV). Whatever the symptom, they know that they need more of the Lord in their ministry.

Death And Dying

When the chief priests and the Pharisees heard Jesus' parables, they knew he was talking about them. They looked for a way to arrest him, but they were afraid of the crowd because the people held that he was a prophet. Matt. 21:45-46 NIV

Jesus was put to death by the Pharisees. They used their authority and manipulated the Roman authorities to condemn Him. He had violated the Law in their eyes and had influence with the people. The Pharisees believed that they had to save God's Kingdom from this infidel and His heresies. Jesus' unmitigated truth threatened men "chosen" by God. He threatened them and what they thought was sacred. All of it was vile in God's sight. When the time was right, Jesus surrendered to them. He surrendered to the Flesh. It was not the Devil who killed Jesus, although he may have inflamed and incited the Flesh to act. It was the Adamic Nature (Flesh) that was at work in the Pharisees from whom Jesus had come to redeem men. Jesus, therefore, surrendered to the Adamic Nature and its hostility toward God, so we could be redeemed from it. He became despised and shamed and took on all the separation from God that is inherent in the Fallen Nature. Jesus' death is an example to us of what the death and defeat of the Old Man is like. Just as the process of sanctification follows a pattern as illustrated by the Children of Israel's journey, the process of death of the Adamic Nature is patterned by Jesus' death. The following are the steps of Jesus' death which are parallel to the steps in the death of the Adamic Nature.

Palm Sunday

It would seem unusual to include such a glorious event as part of the process of dying, but it is an important part of the pattern. When Jesus entered Jerusalem, it was a symbol of his Lordship and authority to reign. It is the equivalent of a prophetic word to us. It spoke of what was to come. Before God does something in our lives, He will give us a revelation of what He is going to do. In the case of the Children of Israel, He told them that He was going to take them to the Promised Land. It was a place filled with prosperity and abundance and peace. He did not tell them what it would take to get there. He wanted them to understand what it was that they were going for. We often think when we are at this stage, that we now have, or will soon have, what we are promised, but it is only the first stage of the Process. Much of the preaching today is powerfully prophetic, proclaiming the great victories of the Church. They are in fact preparing us for the struggle of death. God whets our appetite for the good things He has for us. Little do we know what it will take to enter into that blessing. The Kingdom treasure can only be had through death. We see the beginning and the end but not what is in between; it is easier to say "*yes*" to God that way.

Last Supper

The Last Supper was the preparation for the changes that would occur in His disciples in the next few days. Jesus used this time to prepare the disciples for what was to come, after His resurrection. He modelled to them the humility of leadership by washing their feet. By doing this, He also demonstrated His love and complete commitment, even unto death, for the Church. He was also very intimate with those around Him. There was no public meeting, just the twelve disciples. When we are in the process of death, the last supper stage is a short season of intimate fellowship and reassurance from the Father that we are on the right path before death becomes obvious.

Gethsemane

The garden was a place of sorrow. Death was imminent and there was at this time a period of sorrow, melancholy, even sadness which precedes the death of an area of the Flesh. It is also a place of choice. There is still time to turn back, but if we choose to face the death, this stage will become "sweet sorrow". Just as Jesus was deserted by the disciples at this stage, we are either deserted emotional or physically or feel deserted spiritually. We have to die alone; no one can comfort us or help us at this stage in the process of dying.

The Cross

The cross is death, and no human being will give himself over to death. Everything within us is raging against the situation, but at the same time we continue to move forward into it like a bug drawn to a lamp. It may seem self-destructive, and in a manner of speaking, it is. In death, there is an emptiness, and spiritual darkness. This darkness is not an evil darkness. It is just the absence of light. On two occasions I experienced a sense of torment in my spirit during this time which lasted several days. These experiences (the darkness and torment) gave me a glimpse of what awaits a person who does not know the salvation found in Jesus.

Resurrection

When resurrection happens it is almost a surprise. It is as if someone unexpectedly turns on the lights. We feel a wonderful revelation and sweet intimacy and fellowship with Jesus. We experience a deep humility which seems so natural and effortless. We feel grateful, and repentant for our rebellion and rage against God that is inherent in the process of death of the Flesh. Most of all, we have a revelation and an awareness that we are now standing on higher spiritual ground. It feels like a spiritual high point, where all that was suffered was nothing compared to the treasure that is now suddenly available to us. It is the glorious moment that was "prophesied" on Palm Sunday, fulfilled. The death that has transpired has put another nail in the coffin of the Old Man and all of Heaven rejoices. From that day on, we have a new freedom and perspective on the Kingdom. We also have a new spiritual authority. Things never seen before in the Scripture or in the Kingdom seem obvious or come by revelation. This does not mean we will never sin again, but it does mean we have gained another level of authority in the Kingdom, and over the Flesh in our lives. With it comes revelations of understanding, knowledge, and wisdom which now take up residence in our Heart. These are treasures we own and which will be taken with us into eternity. These treasures are the foundation and pre-qualification for our ruling the universe and the earth with Jesus in the Age to Come.

We were therefore buried with him through baptism into death in order that, just as Christ was raised from the dead through the glory of the Father, we too may live a new life, if we have been united with him like this in his death, we will certainly also be united with him in his resurrection. For we know that our old self was Crucified with him so that the body of sin might be done away with, that we should no longer be slaves to sin— because anyone who has died has been freed from sin. Romans 6:4-7 NIV

Chapter Eight

Stage Three: The Seven Nations

When the LORD your God brings you into the land you are entering to possess and drives out before you many nations — the Hittites, Girgashites, Amorites, Canaanites, Perizzites, Hivites and Jebusites, seven nations larger and stronger than you-- and when the LORD your God has delivered them over to you and you have defeated them, then you must destroy them totally. Make no treaty with them, and show them no mercy. Do not intermarry with them. Do not give your daughters to their sons or take their daughters for your sons, for they will turn your sons away from following me to serve other gods, and the LORD's anger will burn against you and will quickly destroy you. This is what you are to do to them: Break down their altars, smash their sacred stones, cut down their Asherah poles and burn their idols in the fire. For you are a people holy to the LORD your God. The LORD your God has chosen you out of all the peoples on the face of the earth to be his people, his treasured possession. Deut. 7:1-6 NIV

God led Israel into the Promised Land to defeat many nations, but in particular there were seven which He specifically named and wanted deposed. These nations were incompatible with the purposes of God. There could be no compromise or treaties with them because they would take Israel away from following the Lord. He commanded them to destroy them completely and show no mercy. This might seem like a harsh measure to destroy these nations which were occupying the land. It is, however, symbolic of the resolve we must have when dealing with the "nations of our Heart". These Seven Nations represent the motives of the Heart. God judges us by our Heart, so the motive we have for doing something is as important as what we do. Our Heart is spirit and if what we do is corrupted by the motives of the Flesh then we are like the Pharisees who are clean outside, but filthy inside (Matt. 23:27). This portion of the Process focuses on transforming us so we no longer strive to get our Heart needs met through our own works. The Father wants to meet our emotional and spiritual needs so we do not have to strive to get them met through efforts that don't work and from things that don't satisfy.

Motives And Needs

When we were created by God, He placed in us basic needs which could only be fulfilled by Him. The First Adam had all his needs met by God in the Garden of Eden. When the fall came, man was separated from his God and His source of supply for those needs. The Garden of Eden was described as a lush and bountiful place in which there was no need. A garden is often used as a symbol for the spiritual Heart of man. In Jeremiah 31, we are given a promise that the garden of our Heart would again have abundant provision.

They will come and shout for joy on the heights of Zion; they will rejoice in the bounty of the LORD—the grain, the new wine and the oil, the young of the flocks and herds. They will be ***like a well-watered garden,*** *and they will sorrow no more.* Jeremiah 31:12 NIV

The emotional/spiritual needs which God placed in us were intended to be met by Him. The Old Nature, of course, does not have access to God's provision for these needs. As long as the Adamic Nature is alive in us, it will struggle to meet those needs by its own efforts. Jesus accused the Pharisees of being "white-washed sewers". He was saying that on the outside they appeared to be doing all the right things, but He could see their motives for doing these things. Their Hearts were motivated to do the right thing for their own benefit. They could not give unconditional love out of a pure Heart. We may think we are doing the right thing for the right reason, but we cannot see our Heart. It is deceptive and can easily hide or justify our motive. "Good works" are considered dead, because they are an attempt by the Flesh to acquire or earn the approval and acceptance of God. But of course we can't. Only love will justify us through grace. The Old Man cannot give or receive love. Therefore, if we are to be prepared for ministry we must first have the "nations" of our motives crucified, and allow the Father to meet all our needs so that when we minister, we can do it with no expectation of personal gain. If our needs are met, we can enter into relationships and ministry with only the motive of **love**. We can freely give because all our needs are met by God. When our Heart motive for ministry is love, it disarms the skeptics, the wounded, and the abused. As more and more Believers are set free of the bondage of the Flesh, we will see more dramatic healings. Diseases and conditions which rarely give way to prayer will become commonly healed.

A malicious man disguises himself with his lips, but in his heart he harbours deceit. Though his speech is charming, do not believe him, for seven abominations fill his heart. Proverbs 26:24-25 NIV

Ministry done in the Flesh appears to be good and right, but when measured by God, it is fruitless. It tickles the mind and moves the emotions, but it does not touch the spirit of man. Jesus said that giving a cup of cold water to someone out of love will not go without its reward (Matt. 10:42). On the other hand, a huge high profile ministry could be reaching millions, but it may be ministering out of the motives of the Flesh and for this there is no reward. The work will be burned up with all the other works of the Flesh at the coming of the Lord. There are no redeeming qualities about good work done from the motive of the Flesh for the person who is doing the ministry. It does not please God and there is no reward for it. God will not share His glory with another. He puts us through this Process for this very reason.

God judges the motives of the Heart. He sees what we cannot see. He sees why we are doing something. When we minister with a Heart's desire for acceptance, respect, position, or recognition, we have our reward in this life (Matt. 6:1-2). We become what God called Israel before He redeemed her. He called her a harlot working for her pay (Hosea 9:1). We are not harlots. We are the Bride of Christ and He will save us from ourselves. Agape love is unconditional love which can only come from God. It is only available to us through the New Spirit Man which has been resurrected at the death of the Old Man. Jesus gave freely to all people without any intention of receiving anything from them in return. His needs were completely met by God. Jesus has made provision for us to have all our needs met by God, as well.

The Church has turned many people from God because the most visible ministries (on television) have been blatant about expecting to receive people's financial support in return for ministry. How can we prove that the Church truly loves people "unconditionally" if ministry is just like any other business transaction? The shepherds are merciless in their "extractions" of money from the faithful. To even the simplest of minds, it is obviously "ministry with a motive". Jesus disarmed people of their fears of being taken advantage of by His pure love for them. He gave to them but not because He wanted to fill His Church so He would look good, or would be able to make the mortgage payment. He didn't heal people, then put them on a mailing list with appeals for monthly "gifts". There is nothing wrong with mailing lists in themselves, but the motives of this kind of ministry are seriously in question. There are millions of people's destinies at stake, and we must do as Paul did and find a way to be in a position to give freely without need for or expectation of anything in return. If the Church is judged guilty by the heathen, then how much more by a holy God?

When we are subtly and not so subtly attempting to get our needs met by our own efforts, we are always at work. There is no rest. Nothing that the Flesh can do to meet our needs will ever satisfy. The Flesh is a hard taskmaster. There is no end to its pursuits. There is never enough. Jesus said, "*His yoke is easy and His burden is light*" (Matt. 11:30). He is the Prince of Peace because when He meets our needs we are satisfied and at complete rest. David describes this as being like a weaned child at his mother's breast (Psalms 131:2). He understood the contentment we feel when we have our needs met by God. There is nothing wrong with having our needs met. God created us with a hunger in our Heart so that He could meet that hunger. What is evil, however, is that when we are not completely dead in the Flesh, we will attempt to meet those needs through our own manipulation, striving, and conniving. Some people are very obvious about it, some people are very sophisticated. The more religious we get, the more we tend to suppress our real motives. We don't hide anything from God; we only deceive ourselves.

The reaction to the Wilderness is generally fear. At Jericho a war rages between the Flesh and the Spirit which causes confusion. In the Seven Nations stage of the Process, there is a great deal of anger. Job experienced this process of sanctification and his reactions were documented by his friends. They wrote this about him:

Why has your heart carried you away, and why do your eyes flash, so that you vent your rage against God and pour out such words from your mouth? "What is man, that he could be pure, or one born of woman, that he could be righteous? If God places no trust in his holy ones, if even the heavens are not pure in his eyes, how much less man, who is vile and corrupt, who drinks up evil like water! Job 15:12-16 NIV

This stage of the death of the Flesh is a violent, spiritual battle. The motives of man are at the core of his Heart, and to expose these deep areas of his being takes some dramatic circumstances. Invariably, this deep work causes some painful and extreme reactions. Each area is like a stronghold which must be broken down and, when finally exposed, put to death. It is the circumstances that expose our Heart that are the most painful to endure for the Believer. The Flesh does not give up easily and will fight against the humbling and exposing circumstances, trying to avoid the inevitable. The Body does the same thing when faced with physical death. When God is dealing in this area of the Heart, there will be manifestations of anger that rise up from the Flesh which can surprise and overwhelm us. This is all part of the Process. God is not offended when the Flesh manifests its hatred for Him. Even Jesus, being fully man, accused God on the cross of forsaking Him (Matt. 27:46). It is part of the process of the death of the Flesh.

He has preserved our lives and kept our feet from slipping. For you, O God, tested us; you refined us like silver. You brought us into prison and laid burdens on our backs. You let men ride over our heads; we went through fire and water, but you brought us to a place of abundance. Psalms 66:9-12

The Needs (7 Nations) Of The Heart of Man

1. Love And Acceptance

"*Without love we are nothing*" is the theme of many songs and observation confirms this to be true. We were created to love and be loved. The human Heart seeks unconditional love. Teenagers rebel when they discover that their parents' love is "flawed". We quickly recognise the difference between what is pure love and what is selfishness, or infatuation. Nothing but pure love will satisfy our Heart, even though it doesn't exist on this earth. People can only partially fulfill this need. No matter what we do to get love from people, we will rarely be satisfied by it. The love of the Father is so deep and pure, it not only meets our need for love, but also transforms our being. His love enables and motivates us to love others. It is love that confirms to us our worth. To God, we are of infinite value and the quality of His love tells us who we are - we are Sons and Heirs and Royal Priests of the Kingdom of God (1 Peter 2:9).

2. Intimacy

Hidden in the Heart of every man and woman is the desire to know and to be known. We long to share our lives with others who will understand us. We want to be "connected" emotionally and spiritually to someone whom we can trust with everything we are. When God created man and woman, He designed sex to be for more than procreation. He made sex to be an expression of intimacy. Sex without intimacy is an expression of the Flesh. It is lust. It is taking, rather than giving. Therefore, for sex and intimacy to be what they were meant to be, we must have the lusts of the Flesh crucified and true intimacy with God first; then intimacy is possible with others. Our need for intimacy must be fulfilled in our relationship with God so that we can approach our human relationships without being driven by need. If we can enter relationships with no expectations, we cannot be wounded or disappointed because our only purpose is to give. We can then give unconditionally. This is true and fruitful ministry. It sets the captives free because it meets their needs first, and unconditional love disarms their defences. It is this kind of ministry with which Jesus won our Hearts.

Our walk with God should be open, honest, and without deception. This is a requirement of intimacy. If we will share our most secret thoughts with Him and become fully exposed, we will enter a deeper level of intimacy. When the Flesh and its hostility to God is alive, a barrier arises which prevents us from jumping up on His lap and bearing our soul. The Flesh's struggle to acquire intimacy must be completely destroyed in order for us to have true spiritual intimacy.

3. Honour, Respect And Purpose

"*Without a vision the people perish*" (Proverbs 29:18). Without purpose, we are unmotivated and disoriented. Most of us will turn to dissipation (wasting excesses) if we have no purpose in life. We crave honour and purpose because it gives order and meaning to an otherwise meaningless existence. To discover our purpose and call is to discover in part who we are. It answers the important question, "*why am I here?*". Only God can speak our purpose to us. Only He can "call us". Only God can speak destiny to us. We could choose a career in the most humanitarian effort, and never find the Heart fulfilment we would experience when we run the race and complete the task for which we were called, by God, at the foundation of the earth. We could be successful in OUR endeavour but unfulfilled in the fullest sense at the Heart level. In God's eyes, we would be unfruitful. Our destiny is a gift from God. In the movie: "Chariots of Fire", Eric Liddle said, "*I was created to run. It was God who made me fast, and when I run I feel God's glory.*" Eric was in God's ministry, not his own. Our Heart lusts after the adulation of people. Until we are dead to this desire for honour and respect of people, we cannot fully receive the honour of the Father. Our reward for completing our call will be God honouring us before all the throngs of Heaven with "*well done good and faithful servant*" (Matt. 25:21 NIV).

In a loud voice they sang: "Worthy is the Lamb, who was slain, to receive power and wealth and wisdom and strength and honour and glory and praise!" Rev. 5:12 NIV

Jesus completed the task for which He came to earth. He humbled Himself even unto death and defeated Death (the Flesh), the Devil and the world. He was worthy to receive from the Father the seven "rewards" of Revelations 5 verse 12. Jesus was worthy to receive honour because He completed the purpose (call) that was set before Him. Honour and respect are linked to our purpose. We must have a purpose and we crave, out of our very nature, to be good at something, and to be honoured and respected for it. It is not wrong to seek honour. It is good in itself, but it is how and where we receive it that makes it either evil or good. God calls us, and He gives us gifts and talents which enable us to do our ministry and to be honoured by Him for our obedience. If in our Heart we use our talents and gifts to feed our need for honour and respect, rather than to serve the Father, it is spiritual adultery.

4. Power And Position

When God created the earth, He gave man dominion over it. He was empowered to rule the earth and all that was in it (Genesis 1:28). God did that to meet man's needs for power and position. When God gave man this responsibility, He also gave him the power to rule. Nothing makes a person more "sick" than to have a responsibility and not the power to be responsible. Man was created to take rulership over his domain. This is not presumptuous. It was how he was made by God. A simple expression of this is the common desire for home ownership or enterprise. It gives us authority over our domain. In the business world and in the world in general, it is obvious what the work of the Flesh has done. The manifestation of greed and fear, manipulation and all forms of wickedness are rampant everywhere. They are the manifestations of the illness and self-destruction of humanity. The work of the Flesh brings pain, suffering, sickness, and destruction wherever it reigns. God's intention is to empower us with the Holy Spirit. He has given us power over all the works of the Devil, sin, sickness, death, and over the whole earth.

5. Provision, Wealth, And Prosperity

The need for provision, wealth, and prosperity is operational on all three levels of a human being. We require provision for our needs on the physical, emotional, and spiritual dimension. We cannot provide for ourselves. God must make provision for us on all levels, for us to have abundance, and to go forward in our calling. It is out of our prosperity that we can minister. We have a requirement, therefore, for His provision and an intrinsic desire for abundance. The Garden of Eden was the ultimate in abundance; it was God's provision for Adam and Eve's physical, emotional and spiritual needs. Unbelievers seek this same abundance. The world holds a misguided belief that if we make enough money we will be happy. If we believe the folly that money will satisfy, then why do we never have enough? Does anyone win the lottery and refuse the money because they already have enough? It will never happen. Will more money make us more happy? No, this is the lust of the Flesh. It can never be satisfied, and it never satisfies. It is a substitute for the wealth found only in the Spirit of God. Many Christians live with one foot in the Kingdom and one foot in the world. We are compelled to pursue the wealth of this world. In our business life, we may operate with more integrity than the world, but our goal is the same - increase, expand, get more. The lust of the Flesh for wealth is greed. Greed is never satisfied. When Christians seek this abundance in the Flesh, it is "religious greed". Even ministries manifest this drive to become bigger, and to do more, and it is not the Spirit in most cases. It is the lust of the Flesh. Jesus promised that we would be fruitful to the point of abundance, if we abide in Him (John 15:4). We don't have to do anything but obey Him, and He will do the rest, through us.

6. Home And Security

One of the main elements of the promise of the Promised Land was that it was a place of rest and security. There were no wild animals to fear, nor would there be any hostile nations who would threaten Israel (Deut. 25:19). In order for us to be at rest, we must not have fear of attack or calamity. We need a place of safety and retreat. Jesus said; "*come unto me and I will give you rest.*" (Matt. 11:28) There is no rest in this world. Crime, natural disasters, and accidental tragedy are commonplace. There can be no security for those who do not know the "keeping power" of Jesus Christ. Our Heart must be transformed to know that nothing can separate us from the love and protection He has for His people. The Heart of Flesh cannot receive the love which assures us and brings us to peace. We cannot blossom in our giftedness or move forward in our call if our primary relationships, our home, and our church are not safe places. When our Heart is transformed, we are no longer vulnerable to the fear of attack and accident because we know in our Heart that we are completely in God's hands.

7. The Will

God has endowed man with the inalienable right of choice. We were created with the need and power of self-direction. Whole nations have languished when their right of personal choice has been taken away by oppressive governments, as was the case in the Soviet Union in the past. As dangerous as it was, God created us to have choice, even in the Garden where every need was met. But the power of choice is both a blessing and a curse because we were created with a will. We can be self-willed and unyielding, or surrendered to God. If we do not have our will surrendered to Christ, we will go astray from Him. If we give up our will and allow God to direct us completely we will find life eternal and abundant, and that it will produce fruitfulness for the Kingdom through the Holy Spirit. Some people "lose it" when they are out of control. This is the fruit of the unredeemed will. It causes pain for those around them. When Jesus came to Gethsemane, He reaffirmed His surrender to the Father. "*Not my will, but thy will be done*" (Luke 22:42). When we come to Jesus for salvation, we surrender to Him not only as Saviour but also as Lord. The Process is tumultuous. It is difficult to fully explain the Process in specifics because God does His work of redemption differently in each person. The needs of man are at the very core of his being. They are part of his spirit, and they can only be met spirit to Spirit. The Father is our source for all our needs. He is "life" which flows to us because of Jesus through the Holy Spirit.

The Flesh motives are an abomination to God. He hates them, because they keep His people from His provision. When His people are cut off from His provision, they attempt to get their needs met by their own efforts, which leads them to evil. The conquering of the Seven Nations brings provision, rest, and fruitfulness in Jesus Christ.

He is like a tree planted by streams of water, which yields its fruit in season and whose leaf does not wither. Whatever he does prospers. Psalms 1:3 NIV

Jesus Acquired For Us
Jesus' death acquired for us the "legal" right to the promises and provision of God. We are saved when we claim those promises, made by Jesus, as our "right" to eternal and abundant life. In order to enter salvation, a spiritual death occurs. We must be humbled and come to the realization that only Jesus can save us from our "hell". This humbling is a death of the Old Man's pride and independence and rebellion against God. Each area of salvation that the Holy Spirit will lead us into will require a death. Some deaths are more difficult than others. In some areas of our lives, there is a generational history of grace, and in other areas there are generations of no grace due to sinful attitudes which have been handed down parent to child. When the Holy Spirit is putting to death an area that has been under grace, it is much easier to respond to God and allow Him Lordship over that area of the Heart. It is still a death but it is not as difficult. However, when a "nation" of the Heart is being conquered, it will cause "extreme" reactions.

When Jesus died for us on the cross, He acquired all of the needs which were mentioned before. The acquisition of our need is demonstrated by Jesus giving up this area of His life (death) so we can receive His provision. By doing this, He acquired the legal right for us to receive what He died to provide. It does not mean we automatically receive it. We just have the right to receive it.

Jesus took on the Adamic Nature at the cross and died for the redemption of all men. He gained Lordship over the Flesh in every area, thereby acquiring for us the right to meet these needs by the power of the Holy Spirit. Scripture gives a view of Jesus' death and our promise.

1. Jesus acquired for us **Love and Acceptance.**
Jesus' death: "*....My God, my God, why hast thou forsaken me?*" Matt. 27:46
Our promise: "*...nor height, nor depth, nor any other creature, shall be able to separate us from the love of God, which is in Christ Jesus our Lord. Nothing shall separate us from the Love of Christ.*" Rom. 8:39

2. Jesus acquired for us **Intimacy.**
Jesus' death: left the intimacy of the Trinity in Heaven. "*For I have come down from heaven.....*" John 6:38
Our promise: that we may become the Bride of Christ "*I am jealous for you with a godly jealousy. I promised you to one husband, to Christ, so that I might present you as a pure virgin to him.*" 2 Cor. 11:2 NIV
"*...Come, I will show you the bride, the wife of the Lamb.*" Rev. 21:9 NIV

3. Jesus acquired for us **Honour, Respect, Purpose:**
Jesus' death: "*He is despised and rejected of men; a man of sorrows, and acquainted with grief: and we hid as it were our faces from him; he was despised, and we esteemed him not.*" Isa. 53:3
Our Promise: "*But ye are a chosen generation, a royal priesthood, a holy nation,....*" 1 Peter 2:9

4. Jesus acquired for us **Power and Position:**
Jesus' death: *Who, being in the form of God, thought it not robbery to be equal with God: ......he humbled himself, and became obedient unto death, even the death of the cross.* Philippians 2:6-9
Our promise: *"He has give us power over serpents and scorpions and over all the power of the enemy and nothing by any means shall hinder us."* Luke 10:19 NIV

5. Jesus acquired for us **Provision, Wealth and Prosperity:**
Jesus' death: *"...though he was rich, for your sake he became poor, that through his poverty you may become rich."* 2 Cor. 8:9 NIV
Our promise: *"And my God will meet all your needs according to his glorious riches in Christ Jesus."* Philippians 4:19 NIV

6. Jesus acquired for us **Home and Security:**
Jesus' death: *"Foxes have holes and birds have nests, but the Son of Man has nowhere to lay His head."* Matt. 8:20 NIV
Our promise: *"In my Father's house there are many mansions ......I go to prepare a place for you."* John 14:2

7. Jesus acquired for us **our Will:**
Jesus' death: *"...not my will, but thy will be done."* Luke 22:42
Our Promise: *"As a result, he does not live the rest of his earthly life for evil human desires, but rather for the will of God."* 1 Peter 4:2 NIV

Our Ministry
Then he called the crowd to him along with his disciples and said: "If anyone would come after me, he must deny himself and take up his cross and follow me. Mark 8:34, NIV

And anyone who does not carry his cross and follow me cannot be my disciple. Luke 14:27 NIV

Not only is the process of sanctification our preparation for ministry, it **IS** our ministry. We cannot be a disciple of Jesus unless we are prepared to take up our own cross and die as He did. We are called to follow in His footsteps. We are called to do what He has done. Jesus had His needs met from God, but for the sake of His ministry to this world, He gave up His provision and died. By doing this, He acquired for us provision for our needs. Our call to take up our cross and follow Jesus is a call to the cross. It is not a physical cross of physical death because the authority to defeat the Adamic Nature has already been won. Our death will allow us to acquire blessing and grace for others. This is our ministry to the world. If we lay down our life (die) for the sake of others, we can acquire grace (through our humility- death) for those to whom we are called to minister. If we give up our life and die to the Flesh, we shall find it and be like Him.

Our Cross/Our Preparation for Ministry
The following is our call to death and the promise made to those to whom we are called to minister.

1. The Cross of **Love and Acceptance:**
The Believer's Death: *And the brother shall deliver up the brother to death, and the father the child: and the children shall rise up against their parents, and cause them to be put to death, and ye shall be hated of all men for my name's sake: but he that endureth to the end shall be saved.* Matt. 10:21
The call to fruitful ministry: *This is my commandment, That ye love one another, as I have loved you.* John 15:12 *By this shall all men shall know that ye are my disciples, if ye have love one to another.* John 13:35,

2. The Cross of **Intimacy**

The Believer's Death:, *And every one that hath forsaken houses, or brethren, or sisters, or father, or mother,* ***or wife****, or children, or lands, for my name's sake, shall receive a hundredfold, and shall inherit everlasting life.* Matt. 19:29

The call to fruitful ministry: *For I am jealous over you with godly jealousy: for I have espoused you to one husband, that I may present you as a chaste virgin to Christ.* 2 Cor. 11:2, *That there should be no schism in the body; but that the members should have the same care one for another. And* ***whether one member suffer, all the members suffer with it****; or one member be honoured, all the members rejoice with it. Now ye are the body of Christ, and members in particular.* 1 Cor. 12:25-27,

3. The Cross of **Honour, Respect and Purpose:**

The Believer's Death: *We are fools for Christ's sake, but ye are wise in Christ; we are weak, but ye are strong; ye are honourable, but we are despised.* 1 Cor. 4:10,

The call to fruitful ministry: *"ye are honourable, but we are despised"* 1 Cor. 4:10

4. The Cross of **Power and Position**

The Believer's Death: *If others be partakers of this power over you, are not we rather? Nevertheless* ***we have not used this power; but suffer all things, lest we should hinder the gospel of Christ.*** 1 Cor. 9:12 *To the weak I became weak, to win the weak. I have become all things to all men so that by all possible means I might save some.* 1 Cor. 9:22 *That is why, for Christ's sake, I delight in weaknesses, in insults, in hardships, in persecutions, in difficulties. For when I am weak, then I am strong.* 2 Cor. 12:10

The call to fruitful ministry: *For the kingdom of God is not in word,* ***but in power****.* 1 Cor. 4:20

5. The Cross of **Provision, Wealth and Prosperity:**
The Believer's Death: *As sorrowerful, yet always rejoicing; as poor, yet making many rich; as having nothing yet possessing all things.* 2 Cor. 6:10,
The call to fruitful ministry: *Then Peter said, Silver and gold have I none; but such as I have give I thee: In the name of Jesus Christ of Nazareth rise up and walk.* Acts 3:6,

6. The Cross of **Home and Security**
The Believer's Death: *Even unto this present hour we both hunger, and thirst, and are naked, and are buffeted, and have no certain dwelling place; And labour, working with our own hands: being reviled, we bless; being persecuted, we suffer it:* 1 Cor. 4:11,
The call to fruitful ministry: *For whosoever shall give you a cup of water to drink in my name,* ***because ye belong to Christ****, verily I say unto you, he shall not lose his reward.* Mark 9:41

7. The Cross of **the Will:**
The Believer's Death: *You need to persevere so that when you have done the will of God, you will receive what he has promised.* Hebrews 10:36, NIV
The call to fruitful ministry: *The world and its desires pass away, but the man who does the will of God lives for ever.* 1 John 2:17 NIV

The Cross
The cross is a place of pain and suffering. Job suffered and came to a revelation of who God was. (Job 42:5) He also learned His ways of doing things. He faced those who in their arrogance thought they knew God and what was going on with Him. They condemned him. Their redemption was in Job's prayer. He had acquired the grace for them to enter a new truth. He suffered so they could both come into new truth. Paul's suffering and death of his Flesh was for the sake of establishing the gentile Church. Death is the start of

new life. It acquires the grace necessary to enter new truth and new life. Jesus was different than the prophets of old. He brought not only truth but also grace. It is through His humbling and death (acquisition of grace) we can enter truth. Our call to be like Him starts with our own humbling and death. The work of a prophet is to point the way and to intercede for the Church to acquire new truth and spiritual authority by grace.

The Army In Boot Camp

It is difficult to anticipate what God is going to do, but it would appear that He has called a great number of prophets into the Wilderness. Many of these have been in the Process for many years. They have been called to proclaim prophetically the "call" to the Church that it is entering the season of refining. The Process typically takes many years to complete. It is unclear how God will accelerate the Process but He is going to escalate the number of people who are in the Wilderness and the rate at which they move through the various stages. It would appear that this is the season of God calling people out of the world's system and into the Wilderness. Believers everywhere, knowingly or unknowingly are talking about the Wilderness from an experiential point of view. This was not true 10 years ago. Today, however, the Process is a real experience for many of us. We are in it, whether we understand it or not. A year before I entered the Wilderness, a friend had a vision for me. It was of a plant growing in the desert. There was no source of nourishment yet it was surviving very nicely. I believe many people will be called out of their jobs and "places" to follow the Holy Spirit through the Wilderness and into a spiritual Promised Land. They will minister to the Church and the world with an exciting and powerful authority which in the past has only rarely been seen. These people will be the most unlikely people for this ministry by the Church's standards. They will, however, carry with them such a mantle of authority they will be accepted. They will be part of God's restructuring of the Church which will become a true representation of the Body of Jesus Christ. The prophets of old suffered persecution and humiliation and so will these **"Forerunners"**, but it will not stop them. There will be chaos and turmoil in the Church but in what appears to be conflict and disorder, God will reform His people and His Church. In spite of the chaos, it will be a glorious time where Jesus will take His Lordship in a more complete way over His Church.

Our Threefold Redemption

Sanctification is an ongoing process. But there are specific times and seasons of an intense work of the Holy Spirit. These seasons are identifiable, usually in hindsight, but nonetheless they are distinguishable, specific, and systematic. We are called to be redeemed in three areas of our life, the first being our relationship with the Father; the second, our ministry to our family; and third, our ministry to the Body of Christ and to the world. When the valiant men finally defeated the Seven Nations, their wives, children and livestock were the benefactors of the abundance of the Promised Land. They fought and defeated the nations on behalf of their families and their possessions. *Husbands, love your wives, just as Christ loved the church and gave himself up for her.* (Eph. 5:25) The husband is the High Priest of the home and he is called to die in his ministry to his wife and family so that they can enter into the abundance of God. The wife is called to die in order to have a fruitful ministry to the children. Because we are Kings and Priests we are called to die and acquire grace for those for whom we are called to serve in Christ.

God is building an army of Believers who are dead to the works of the Flesh. They will have the full armor of Christ which is spoken of in Ephesians 6:11. All of the armor described there is the armor we acquire when we allow the Spirit to bring death to the Adamic Nature in us. We are enabled to walk in the Spirit and thereby not fulfill the lusts of the Flesh. We are endowed with authority to pull down strongholds. We can do ministry from a Heart motivated by pure love. We will find our personal peace, identity, and prosperity in Christ. We have learned warfare against the Devil and his works in the world. Now, we must learn how to defeat the Flesh. When the Flesh is dead, the Devil will have nothing with which to tempt us. Riches, fame, and success, are no lure to the one who has given these up, and who is free of the love of them. In the heat of the battle against the works of the Flesh and the Devil, there will be nothing that he can do to defeat us. Jesus started a spiritual revolution which has continued and prospers to this day. His death has brought new life to billions of people. The Church is called to be like Him. He is preparing millions of sanctified Spirit-walking-warriors on the earth for the final hour of this world as we know it. No devil in hell, nor work of the Flesh will be able to stand before that army of God. He will redeem us. He will armor us. We will know the intimate fellowship of Christ in our suffering and death. He will captain us, just as He came to Israel in the Wilderness as the "Captain of The Lord of Hosts" (Joshua 5:14). We will be the fruitful vine who abides (lives) and draws all our sustenance from Jesus (John 15:4-8). We will be the spotless Bride of Christ who has been fully prepared to rule and reign with Christ in the Age to Come. We will be fully His, and He will be fully ours. We will be worthy to receive all rewards from the Father because we have overcome the Flesh, the Devil, and the world. (Rev. 11:18).

They will make war against the Lamb, but the Lamb will overcome them because he is Lord of lords and King of kings — and with him will be his called, chosen and faithful followers." Rev. 17:14 NIV

"For many are invited, but few are chosen." Matt. 22:14 NIV

Chapter Nine

Resurrection of the Spirit Man

Jesus looked at him and loved him. "One thing you lack," he said. "Go, sell everything you have and give to the poor, and you will have treasure in heaven. Then come, follow me." At this the man's face fell. He went away sad, because he had great wealth. Mark 10:21-22

The journey through the Wilderness is a journey of faith. We cannot see where we are going and we usually don't know where we are. We have to learn to put our hand in Jesus' hand and trust that He is leading us in the right direction. The problem, however, is that this journey does not take just a week, or a month, or a year. It can take years of working through the various stages for our own relationship with God, for our family, and for our ministry. When I began this Process, it was as if I were standing on a cliff and God said, "*go ahead and jump, I will catch you*". The situations in which I found myself were far beyond me. Only God could save me from them, and to some extent He did, but I continued to "free-fall" for years. The difficult situations continued year after year and my prayer for the "good life" never was answered. Throughout the journey, I always thought at each new victory that it was over and things were going to change back to what they used to be, but they never did. I wanted life to be comfortable again, but my security at the time was based on the things of this world. I often wondered how far I would fall before God would catch me. The answer was "right to the bottom". God is only satisfied with the complete destruction of the Flesh in our life. I didn't know where He was taking me but I have now come to appreciate the benefits of His sanctifying work. It is wonderful to not be ruled by the Flesh. The rich young ruler did everything right but was unable to give up the treasure He had on this earth. It was part of his identity and his comfort. He saw it as a loss instead of a gain to be free of what had him bound to this earth and temporal things. It was a devoted thing for Him. He could not do what Jesus told him to do to gain spiritual riches. Even in some Churches, it is seen to be an expression of righteousness to become rich in material possessions. These things only become stumbling blocks to following Jesus. It is a higher honour to be poor in the Kingdom of God because it is freedom. *Listen, my dear brothers: has not God chosen those who are poor in the eyes of the world to be rich in faith and to inherit the kingdom he promised those who love him?* James 2:5

Israel became weary of their labours in Egypt. They were oppressed by Pharaoh and worked as slaves to a merciless nation. Our Egypt is that we are working for the world's system and values. We spend our life energy on things like new cars and houses and boats and furniture and vacations. We believe these things will make us happy. They are part of being acceptable in this society. If we do not have money and signs of wealth, we are considered lazy or a failure. This view is so prevalent in America that it is as dominating inside the Church, as outside it. The concept of poverty as a value to be desired is unheard of in the Church.

It is a shame of the North American Church that its members would spend 25% of their life acquiring shelter. Between taxes and mortgage interest, the world's system and values "steal" more than half of a man's life. We are supposed to be the Lord's, not slaves to bankers and tax collectors. We are to turn our backs on the world's system and leave Egypt for a place of abundance provided for by the Lord. We are no longer to be consumers whose lives are consumed by consumption. We cannot be controlled by our need to be (more) acceptable or our lust for material things. Yet, we do not stop striving for more possessions or more wealth. We are slaves to the lusts of the Flesh. We cannot stop wanting more things or more respect or more power. As we die both spiritually and physically, we let go of the things which are of least value. If we were told that we had only one month to live, we would spend our time on the things of greatest value. We would spend time on our relationship with the Father, our family, and with our friends. We would reprioritize our life and put value where there is the highest reward. Yet in our society, this is seen as irresponsible in any other circumstance but impending death. There is subtle unspoken demand that we be fruitful in this world, and that is measured by our material possessions. Jesus commands us to live our life as if today were our last day here on earth. We know that we will be judged for what we have done with our life. America is an extremely materialistic society. The Church and its members are caught in the materialism of this world, and for the most part, it is materialism that has prevented it from following the Holy Spirit into the Wilderness. The North American Church is like the Rich Young Ruler who was bound by his wealth to temporal values and unable to discard his wealth for the true treasures of the Kingdom of God. The Church believes that if you are prospering financially then you are being blessed by God so you can supply finances to the Church. The accumulation of material wealth is rewarded, encouraged, and applauded. This is a common theme in most evangelical Churches and it is neither sound scripturally or true spiritually. When Jesus said, "*seek first the Kingdom*", He meant that if the treasure of the Kingdom is our first priority in life then the rest of the issues of life would be properly prioritized and that God would take care of them. Anyone can acquire wealth by the Flesh. Putting our material needs in the hands of the Holy Spirit for His provision is our instruction. We are not to make the needs of this life our priority but do everything we can to acquire the treasure of the Kingdom. This is the beginning of walking into the Wilderness and the Process which will free us from the harsh and cruel taskmaster - the Flesh.

The process of death cannot be hurried, manipulated, nor "prayed through". It has to be experienced. It is a walk and the walk is as much a part of the Process as the destination. When our life depends on hearing and doing what the Spirit is saying, we learn the ways of the Spirit. Learning to be led and not to run ahead or resist the Spirit or "kick" against the circumstances instead of addressing the issues in the Spirit, are the wisdom and understanding discovered in the journey. The Holy Spirit becomes our best friend, sometimes our only friend. He is our Comforter, our Teacher, our Cloud by day and Pillar of Fire by night. He is our Life. The journey is a walk in humility. God's values are nothing like our own. He places no value on many of the things we consider valuable. He does not value reputation. He will sacrifice our reputation in order to save us from our bondage. He has little respect for protocol. He will put us in positions where we will have to choose between our reputation and the prompting of the Spirit. He will consume our savings just to make us depend on Him. He will lead us to associate with certain people we may feel uncomfortable with to have us intercede for them. He will lead us into a situation that will "blow up" just to bring death to the Flesh in us. He will cause us to take a position which seems harsh or unpopular in order to expose or discipline someone. The journey is multi-levelled and multidimensional. He is working on us and others at the same time and He accomplishes a lot with every encounter.

From this time many of his disciples turned back and no longer followed him. "You do not want to leave too, do you?" Jesus asked the Twelve. Simon Peter answered him, "Lord, to whom shall we go? You have the words of eternal life". John 6:66-68 NIV

There are times when we would like to run and hide but we know that there is nowhere to go. Once we have tasted the good things of the Kingdom and the love of Jesus, where can we go? The pain we suffer in the Process is often caused by our own fear, unbelief, and rebellion. When the Father is performing open Heart surgery and exposing and putting to death our Flesh, it is painful. It is our *own* Flesh which causes most of our suffering. There is pain and grieving as our Flesh is being put to death. The more we are dead to the Flesh, the less we suffer in its death. This is the manifestation of the full armor of God. If we suffer persecution for doing what the Holy Spirit has led us to do, we rewards us with His presence and peace and joy. When we suffer in the death of our Flesh, it is painful in another way but the reward is righteousness, peace, and joy.

In the Wilderness, it is not uncommon to develop symptoms of anxiety, striving, nervous habits, restlessness, and fear which all characterize God's exposing of our unbelief. He literally drives us into the Wilderness because we would not go there on our own. If we don't understand what is happening and only see the circumstance in the natural and not with God's spiritual objectives, we will struggle to fix the situation rather than cooperate with Him. If we fight against "a God situation" in our life, we only delay the Process. We must face each situation full front and not try to escape it. Everything that happens, happens for a reason. Instead of struggling, we must pursue God for a revelation of the reason He has us in these circumstances. It is more difficult at the beginning of the Journey than it is after we have gained some victories over the Flesh. The Journey does become easier even though the tests and the circumstances become more difficult. Each time we win over the Flesh, we have a clearer view of the values and treasures of the Kingdom and humbling always brings a renewed and deeper intimacy with Jesus.

At Jericho, we feel like we are being pulled in two directions. We experience confusion and inner turmoil. Our self image is on the altar. God may ask if we are willing to look stupid for Him. It is better to look stupid than to be stupid, so we say, "yes". It never feels good to look stupid in the eyes of others. When God is circumcising our Heart, there is a spiritual pain which is the death of the Pride of Life. It can cause depression and alienation from people. At the same time, there may be a closeness to the Lord and other times He may seem like a million miles away. Whatever the circumstance of death of the Flesh that we experience, it is always painful and sends us into emotional turmoil. If we don't hang on to God in these times, we can easily revert to coping (rebellion), or shutting down our emotions. This Process will take us to our limit. We cannot anticipate what we will do when we come to it. The Adamic Nature attempts to make a life of its own outside of God. It is hostile to God. It hates anything that will reveal it or expose the lie that "*it can do it on its own*". It is trying to rule and be like God. It is trying to be the god of our life.

The walls of Jericho represent the barriers to being fully devoted to God. It can be our prideful understanding of the Scriptures. It can be our goals or objectives. It can even be ministry "our way". It is anything that would keep us from following the Holy Spirit. He doesn't lead Believers in the path of conventional wisdom, nor on the road of respectability, or even common sense. Over and over again, we see this modelled in the accounts of peoples' lives in Scripture, yet we haven't really accepted it as the "true Christian lifestyle". If we begin with the Scripture and attempt to understand the Kingdom of God with our human thinking, we become like the Pharisees, "blind guides leading the blind". If we seek the Lord for a revelation of the Kingdom, and Scripture confirms our revelation, then we know we have found the truth about the Kingdom. The Holy Spirit has been appointed our teacher. It is His job to tear down our walls of earthly wisdom and legalistic teaching. Scripture can be used to support and justify what we must do to make God pleased with us. Of course He is pleased with us already and all we must do to follow Him is to walk obedient to the Holy Spirit. For each person following the Holy Spirit, the journey is different. The arguments for such legalistic compliance can make so much sense when we hear the use of Scripture and human wisdom but the test for legalism and idolatry is found in who is ultimately Lord in the issue. If, when all is said and done, the Holy Spirit is not made Lord over the issue in our life, it is not Godly wisdom, it is legalism. We must surrender to His Lordship for our lives in all things. We cannot make rules or theories or principles out of relationship and walking with our God in obedience. Jesus told the Pharisees they were laying heavy burdens on the people by making them subject to their law and rules. It is a burden to be under the Law but a delight to be in a love relationship with God the Father.

The Seven Nations stage of the Process is the most dramatic for symptoms. The conquering of a Nation is a fierce battle and is filled with intense manifestations. The Nations are more like Jesus' death on the cross than any other part of the Process. Just as the physical body does everything it can to avoid death, so the Flesh struggles to overcome the threat to its reign. When the Flesh is threatened, it may strike out at others and God as a way of concealing itself or regaining control. But the enmity is against God, because He is taking control of this area of our life. Anger and frustration are common in this stage because the Flesh rises up when it loses control. Toward the end of the process of this death, there is a feeling of numbness and helplessness, resignation to defeat, discouragement and then finally death. It is a very emotional time. We need to continually confess that God is good even when we hate what is happening to us. He is loving us enough to free us from the things that taint our ministry and oppose our desire for more of the Kingdom. Be thankful that He gives us what we need and not always for what we ask.

The Process of Sanctification

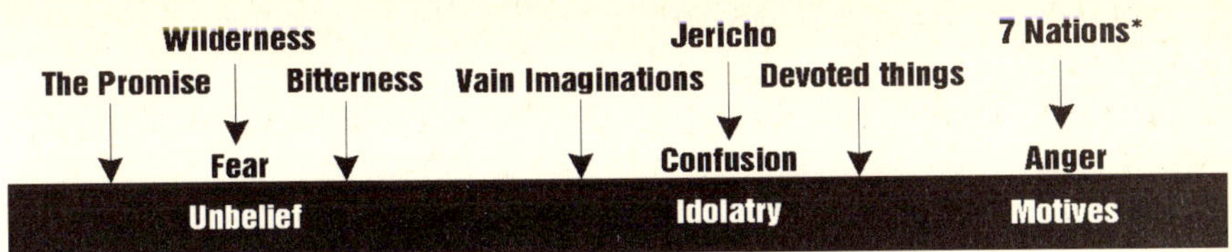

*** The 7 Nations is a three part stage. We go through it once for our relationship with God, once of our ministry to our Family, once for our ministry to the World.**

Choose Life

At times in this process we can feel there is no hope. The Old Man works on our emotions to discourage and confuse. It is hard to choose the life that is in the Holy Spirit and believe that God is good when every fibre in our body is screaming for release from the awful situation we know He has us in. By choosing life, we can literally see our emotions become transformed, and in a matter of minutes see by revelation, God's redeeming work. It is difficult to choose life (the Spirit) rather than death (the Flesh) when we are in the midst of the battle, but we must. We will spend much less time going in circles and make the Process far less painful.

So I say, live by the Spirit, and you will not gratify the desires of the sinful nature. For the sinful nature desires what is contrary to the Spirit, and the Spirit what is contrary to the sinful nature. They are in conflict with each other, so that you do not do what you want. But if you are led by the Spirit, you are not under law. The acts of the sinful nature are obvious: sexual immorality, impurity and debauchery; idolatry and witchcraft; hatred, discord, jealousy, fits of rage, selfish ambition, dissensions, factions and envy; drunkenness, orgies, and the like. I warn you, as I did before, that those who live like this will not inherit the kingdom of God. Gal. 5:16-21 NIV

Advice From Scripture in the Wilderness

Nevertheless, God was not pleased with most of them; their bodies were scattered over the desert. Now these things occurred as examples ***to keep us from setting our hearts on evil things*** *as they did. Do* ***not be idolaters****, as some of them were; as it is written: "The people sat down to eat and drink and got up to indulge in pagan revelry." We* ***should not commit sexual immorality****, as some of them did— and in one day twenty-three thousand of them died. We* ***should not test the Lord****, as some of them did— and were killed by snakes. And* ***do not grumble****, as some of them did—and were killed by the destroying angel. These things happened to them as examples and were written down as warnings for us,* ***on whom the fulfilment of the ages has come.*** 1 Cor. 10:5-11 NIV

Craving Evil Things

Paul specifically wrote to the Corinthians on the matter of the purging and sanctification of the Believer. The story of the Children of Israel was given as instruction so that we would not crave evil things. This has been interpreted as outward acts of immorality, but these are the pursuit of those things that fulfill the Flesh. They are Heart issues. God looks at the Heart and judges it rather than the action. Evil, to God, can be good things done for the wrong reasons as was the case of the Pharisees. Israel did not intentionally rebel, it just happened because it came out of their Heart. Their Heart craved evil things. That was who they were. When we were born again, Jesus took the Heart of Flesh and put it to death and we became the New Man. Therefore, it is not us who sins but the Old Man. We must understand the separation of the Old and the New Man to win the battle against the Flesh. We will avoid condemnation when we do sin and be able to separate the feelings, desires, and thoughts of the Flesh from the Spirit. This allows us to learn and understand the difference between good and evil. Good is to walk in the Spirit; evil is to act out of the Flesh. Even the most reasonable, well meaning, and sensible "wisdom" can be the work of the Flesh. Every situation must be viewed through the eyes of the Holy Spirit to avoid not rebelling against God. Learning obedience in the Wilderness is to submit everything to the Holy Spirit in order to avoid doing things that seem "right" but are the work of a Heart trying to avoid death.

Scripture says that God took the Children of Israel into the Wilderness to teach them that "*man does not live by bread alone, but by every word of God*". (Luke 4:4) Israel was promised a physical land flowing with milk and honey. We are promised the Kingdom of God. The Gospel is often presented as the path to a good life. Paul warned that the Gospel is not a means to material gain (1 Tim. 6:5). It is not the "good life" in the temporal sense. That is idolatry. We "live" out of the Heart. Its spiritual condition determines the quality of our life because we are spirit beings. The temporal things of this life do not produce a quality or fruitful life. They only bind us and burden us and hinder us in our relationship with God. Yet the Flesh Heart lusts after temporal (evil) things and wants to change the Gospel into a way to satisfy the Flesh, instead of destroying it.

Idolatry
When the people saw that Moses was so long in coming down from the mountain, they gathered round Aaron and said, "Come, make us gods who will go before us. As for this fellow Moses who brought us up out of Egypt, we don't know what has happened to him." Aaron answered them, "Take off the gold ear-rings that your wives, your sons and your daughters are wearing, and bring them to me." So all the people took off their ear-rings and brought them to Aaron. He took what they handed him and made it into an idol cast in the shape of a calf, fashioning it with a tool. Then they said, "These are your gods, O Israel, who brought you up out of Egypt." Exodus 32:1-4 NIV

It was a physical god (calf) that Israel had created but it really was no different than the gods we serve in our Heart. God will have no other gods before Him. Idolatry is subtle and its works can appear to be so good to human understanding. When God begins to deal with idolatry in our Heart, we struggle the most with what others will think of us. God may bruise and batter our reputation. We must die to being accepted by others and make obedience to the Holy Spirit more important than what we look like to others. Many of the things that the disciples did brought criticism from prominent persons inside and outside the New Testament Church. If we can let God put to death our desire to be liked by everyone, then we are free to serve Him fully.

If we are rigid in the letter of the Gospel rather than revelation of the Gospel, we are probably in the stubbornness of idolatry. Pursuit of the lusts of the Flesh may take us far from God or only into hidden and subtle habits which drain our spiritual authority and deaden our love and devotion to Christ. When we can't reach God, we substitute a real life-giving relationship based on love and grace for legalistic religion. Paul said that the account of the Children of Israel was given to us so we would not be idolaters. He wanted for us to see that within every Believer is a Heart full of idolatry. We are not to be condemned by that truth but pursue God for freedom, thereby not making the mistake Israel made.

Sexual Immorality

The sexual immorality that Israel committed included joining themselves to other gods. Their sexual immorality lead them to spiritual adultery. They acted immorally in regard to their relationship with God. They sought many different ways to cope with their restless Heart. Coping is a subtle but dangerous inclination in the Process. It causes us to put on hold the work of God. We try to find a way to survive the circumstances, rather than seek God for His redeeming work. It is very easy to fall prey to sexual or spiritual immorality in the Process if we don't walk in humility and surrender to God. When we run up against a wall and we cannot go forward or gain a victory, it is time to pursue God for answers. Sometimes there is nothing for us to do but let Him bring our Heart to the cross and then lead us to victory. However, coping keeps us static and it is rebellion against God. If we are looking for comfort in all the wrong places, it is adultery before God, because we are His Bride.

Test The Lord

Throughout the Process, we are stretched by situations designed specifically to expose and test us. They are meant to take us to our limit. That is how we are strengthened. When we are in the Flesh and not able to see the work of the Holy Spirit for what it is, there is a tendency to feel that God doesn't really love us. This is a common and typical feeling when God is exposing and stretching our faith. If we believe this, we run the risk of putting God on trial with our own test. We may respond to God either verbally or in our Heart, by saying, "*if you really love me you will give me what I want*". Of course God will not respond to that because it would condone the works of the Flesh. If this "trying God" takes us into rebellion against Him, we cannot move forward in the Process. We are cut off from Him, and will stay where we are until we come back to God in humility and confession. It is a work of the Flesh to think we are unloved. God wants us to discern the Flesh so we will not try or rebel against Him in the Process.

Murmuring.

Yea, they despised the pleasant land, they believed not his word: But murmured in their tents, and hearkened not unto the voice of the LORD. Psalms 106:24-25

Another work of the Flesh is complaining about the way God is treating us. Part of the Process is to be left in need by God. Israel complained about God and to Moses about the lack they were in. The Christian life is not a guarantee of a comfortable life. It is not our ***right*** to be provided for abundantly. It is by grace that we have anything of, or from God at all. When we complain about our circumstance, we are accusing God of not loving us or caring for us. When we are in the Process, it is like working out at the spiritual gym; no pain, no gain. He is truly our Lover and Friend. He could not, and would not do anything except what is for our highest good. Even when it doesn't seem like it, He is choosing the best and quickest way to get us from bondage into the Promised Land.

Self Righteousness

It is not because of your righteousness or your integrity that you are going in to take possession of their land; but on account of the wickedness of these nations, the LORD your God will drive them out before you, to accomplish what he swore to your fathers, to Abraham, Isaac and Jacob. Deut. 9:5 NIV

The promises of God are received by the unmerited favour of God. Even after we have surrendered and walked in the Spirit, and chosen to dethrone the Flesh, it is by grace we have received God's deliverance and provision. He has defeated our enemies for us, we haven't. He has given us the blessing and spiritual prosperity of the Kingdom of God by grace. We have these blessings which we did not know existed or know how to find because of the mercy and grace of God. When we hold to that truth, we will remain in the righteousness of Jesus, and not our own.

Conclusion

Dear friends, do not be surprised at the painful trial you are suffering, as though something strange were happening to you. 1 Peter 4:12 NIV

I was in prayer one day when the Lord gave me a vision of a string which had been knotted up into a grapefruit-sized ball. When I asked the Lord what it was, He said, "*in order to unknot the middle knot He had to take the knots out that were there first.*" I had been pursuing Him in prayer for a certain thing. I understood from what He said that He fully intended to answer my prayer but He had an order and a systematic way of doing the work of sanctification. Like building a house, each stage must be completed before the next stage can begin. Because of our personality, woundedness, character traits, and spiritual makeup (weaknesses and strengths) that order is different for each one of us. The "Heart Surgeon" customizes our treatment for each of us. He is an expert at doing the business of redeeming His people. His plan is flawless. His timing is impeccable. He will complete that which He has begun.

Therefore, since we are surrounded by such a great cloud of witnesses, let us throw off everything that hinders and the sin that so easily entangles, and let us run with perseverance the race marked out for us. Let us fix our eyes on Jesus, the author and ***perfecter of our faith****, who for the joy set before him endured the cross, scorning its shame, and sat down at the right hand of the throne of God.* Hebrews 12:1-2 NIV

Three Measures Of Maturity In Christ

Maturity in Christ is judged to be different things in different groups. Each one has their value judgements on what particular character traits are the most important. Many of these character traits are outward expressions of what might be signs of maturity in Christ. Based upon this Process of preparation, the spiritual abilities that God is developing in His Church are those which affect our relationship with Him in difficult times and our ability to remain on the path toward fruitfulness. A summary of these spiritual abilities which God is developing in His Body are as follows:

1. Eyes of Faith: It takes spiritual eyes of faith to see God in the good, bad, and ugly circumstances of our life. In most cases, He is there in the center of our problems with a solution and a role for us to play in it. We are never out of the hands of the Father and our circumstances are meant to teach, discipline, and guide us. The test of maturity is the size of problem we can overcome with trust and faith in God.

2. Saved by Grace: If we know God and His righteousness, then we will realize just how far we fall short of His holiness and depend on His unmerited forgiveness. It is knowing our complete unworthiness that keeps us tolerant of others, thankful, and a channel of grace for fruitful ministry. Without the attitude of an unworthy servant, we cannot see the Kingdom of God or be a fruitful minister in it.

3. Death is the way to Life: The Kingdom of God works opposite to that of the world. We know this is true but only when we live like it is true can we gain the treasure of the Kingdom of God. When we can embrace death with the expectation of great gain, we will understand the Kingdom of God and how Christ transforms us. When we can follow the Holy Spirit into death of the Flesh with joy for the sake of gaining the promises of the Kingdom, we are well on the way to becoming the warriors of God.

These three manifestations of maturity are not things which can be acquired by knowing them, but treasure which can only be had by walking with God. It is in walking with Him that our orientation and perspective of the Kingdom and the Gospel are formed. It is by walking with God that these maturity traits become the foundation upon which we live our lives.

When they saw the courage of Peter and John and realised that they were unschooled, ordinary men, they were astonished and they took note that these men had been with Jesus. Acts 4:13 NIV

No Formulas

When Jesus was transfigured, Peter, James and John wanted to build an altar there to mark the spot and turn it into a religious shrine. Jesus knew that people, in their carnality, would worship the spot where it happened and denied their request. When God does something wonderful for us we want to understand and capture it. The Flesh wants to package it and show others the way to do it, so we can look good. It is our Fallen Nature to want to make a dependent walk with God into a system, and relationship into rules, principles and laws. The solution to whatever our need or desire is, is always in our acquisition of grace through humility. We cannot separate healing or provision from God. They can only be found **in** Him. It is a work of the Flesh to separate what we want or need from God. Our answers are always found in Him. It is simple. We must have the hostility of the Flesh put to death so we can take more of Jesus into our life and in Him there is all that we need. There are no other formulas or teachings or methods to get from God what we need. We need more of Him. We must dive into the pool of the Trinity and be fully immersed in them. We must be transformed by our exposure to their love and holiness, and we will find abundance and freedom far beyond our need or expectation.

Learning To Ask The Right Questions

When we are in the midst of a problem our first response is usually to pray for it to be taken away. If it is sickness or financial trouble or some other problem we may reason that God does not want this in our lives. We interpret the delay in our answer to prayer as our faith being tested. In many situations, this is not the case. More often than not, the delay in our answer to prayer is due to our asking for the wrong solution to our problem. There is a reason for every situation in which we find ourselves. If we ask for its removal rather than the wisdom and direction to overcome it, God does not answer. We should be asking, "*Lord, why am I in this situation?*", "*What are you trying to teach me in it?*",

"How can I cooperate with your purposes in it?", and *"What do you want me to do in the process of your overcoming this situation for me?"*. We cannot choose our own solutions to our problems. We must rely on God and ask Him to solve the problem His way. His way is always better than our way. Therefore, we must confess our inability to work anything out for ourselves. If we become weak, He will become strong for us. We must let God get us out of the situation with as little of our involvement as is possible. He loves us and when He solves our problems, it is always a blessing to us and others.

Learning To Walk In The Spirit

We can either walk by the Scriptures or we can walk by the Holy Spirit. If we walk by the "Word", **we** are in charge. If we walk by the Holy Spirit, **He** is in charge. If we place our life in His hands we will look foolish, because He will lead us into death, and suffering, and humility. For this reason, many have refused to surrender to the Holy Spirit - they don't want to be a failure in the eyes of others. Even when we choose to do the right thing and walk obedient to the Spirit, the Flesh is very deceptive and can easily influence our "hearing" God, especially in the early stages of our walk with Him. This will lead us down dead end paths and we will look foolish again. The Lord uses even these mistakes to teach us, humble us and free us of the Flesh. Nothing can separate us from His love. If we choose to walk in the Spirit, we will make mistakes and they will be embarrassing. Our Flesh will be exposed. It may seem as if we are going around in circles, but Jesus IS in control. There is a high potential for making mistakes when we choose to live our lives by "hearing" God and walking in the Holy Spirit. We must walk with Him and abide in Him if we are to be known by Him. In spite of the risks of putting our lives in the hands of the Holy Spirit, **there is no other life for Believers**.

The Promised Land Is....

The Promised Land represents for us as Believers a number of things which are inherent in the Kingdom of God. When we possess it, we have taken it by force by putting the Flesh under the lordship of the Holy Spirit. Our taking the Kingdom by force is to rise up in the Spirit, choosing life instead of the death and putting the Flesh in submission to the Holy Spirit. This is another aspect of spiritual warfare. The treasures of the Kingdom available to those who conquer the Promised Land are:

1. spiritual authority for our calling and a position of service in the Kingdom,
2. the development of the Fruits of the Spirit which are the foundation of fruitfulness in our ministry,
3. provision for every need,
4. the promises of the Kingdom which are summed up in - love, joy and peace,
5. successful overcoming of the Devil and the Flesh which is the manifestation of the full armor of God,
6. the ability to discern Good (the Spirit) from Evil (the Flesh),
7. greater ability to walk in the Spirit,
8. a Heart of love and compassion - which is to love the lost, the Body of Christ, and the Lord with all of our Heart, mind, and strength and finally,
9. we qualify for the rewards of Revelation 5:12 that Jesus received when He loved not His life unto death which are: power, and riches, and wisdom, and strength, and honour, and glory, and blessing.

Things To Do When You Finish Reading This Book

When the Children of Israel left Egypt, God performed ten miracles specifically to prove to them that He would meet their needs through supernatural events. He told them to write everything down so they would remember all that He did for them. He also told them to remember the Promise and to recount for themselves why they had left Egypt. There is a saying that is not Scripture, but it is wisdom. It is:

"Obstacles are those frightening things we see when we take our eyes off the vision." This expresses what God was trying to do with the Children of Israel when He commanded them to write down what He had done, and was promising to do for them. He wanted them to remember His faithfulness and supernatural ability to meet their needs. He wanted them to focus their attention not on the problems of the day, but on the objective. That is good advice for us. We should write down the things that God has promised us and the miracles of deliverance which He has done so we will not be overwhelmed by the "obstacles". We need to be reminded that nothing can separate us from His love. We should read these testimonies often and recount them to our friends and family. This was David's secret. He remembered the goodness and faithfulness of God and reaffirmed to himself and God that He could trust Him. The Psalms of David in the Wilderness reveal how He was caught up in "obstacles" but was refreshed by a renewed vision of God and His purpose and love for him.

You have made known to me the path of life; you will fill me with joy in your presence, with eternal pleasures at your right hand. Psalms 16:11 NIV

Some readers of this book will discover that they have rebelled against the Lord in this Process. It may have been without understanding that you have squirmed off the sacrificial altar and went on your own way. It is never too late to get back on track. You can turn against the Flesh and agree with God in a simple prayer. You can pour out your Heart of fear and rebellion and ask Him to deliver you. He will take your emotions, sin, and failings and carry them if you ask Him. He is your only true Lover.

Is your walk with God shallow? Is God just a small part of your life? Has your intimacy with Jesus or your love for Him grown cold? Ask the Holy Spirit where you have strayed from the path of life and gone into the ditch. You can ask Him for the treasures of the Kingdom and the abundance and rest of the Promised Land. You have a right to them in Jesus Christ. You can ask Him to put to death your unbelief, idolatry and rebellion and all the hostility of the Flesh. You can choose abundant life or settle for just eternal life. The abundant life (Kingdom of God) is like the "*Pearl of Great Price*". It is worth selling everything you have to get it. It is like exchanging something that is worthless for something that is priceless.

And Jesus said unto him, No man, having put his hand to the plough, and looking back, is fit for the kingdom of God.
Luke 9:62 NIV

...and that we must through much tribulation enter into the kingdom of God.
Acts 14:22 NIV

Humble Yourself

You have a responsibility to act on the knowledge you have received. Now that God has brought understanding of His Process, it would be prudent to take some time to fast and pray about what God wants you to know and understand from this book. He may direct you to reread portions of the text or the entire book, so that He can underscore certain areas to you by the Holy Spirit. Your objective should be to get a revelation from God of what He has for you in this season of your walk with Him. You need a revelation of His work of sanctification in you. Ask Him to reveal your Heart and what the next step is in cooperating with Him in His purging of the Flesh in your life. He may call you to a time of confession and repentance in order for you to get back into the flow of the life and redemption of God. Whatever He requires, do not refuse Him!

Couples

Husbands are commanded to love their wives as Christ loved the Church. (Eph. 5:25) Sometimes this is interpreted as the husband doing everything and anything he can to please his spouse. Although this may be seen by some as a demonstration of this Scripture and godliness, it can become an opportunity for the Flesh. We are being redeemed from the Flesh and must not then make ourselves or our spouse subject to our fleshly desires. As couples, we must agree that we will work toward walking in the Spirit and putting to death those desires which are not from the Holy Spirit. If our spouse is not able to work with us in this way, we must then navigate this area of our journey with a great deal of understanding, prayer, and waiting on the Lord to intervene in His time. This in itself can be a death. If it is possible to work together, however, helping each other discern what is Spirit and what is Flesh can be a powerful and effective method to find our way through the stages of the Wilderness Process.

Our Calling

Some of us know what our true calling is. For most of us, however, it is somewhat unclear. Whether God will reveal specifically what He has for us or not doesn't matter. We should seek as much understanding as we can at this time. For those with a prophetic word, they should pray it, and confess it as truth before God, but leave it in His hands. Prophetic words are for praying and for confirmation after they have been fulfilled. Rarely do we understand prophetic words *before* God brings them into being. We need not worry about achieving our call since it is the Holy Spirit's job to prepare us for our ministry. All we have to do is be obedient to Him day-by-day.

Share This Book

There are so many people who have become stuck in the Wilderness and are like the dying generation of Israel. They do not understand what God is doing in their lives. They have turned away from following the Spirit in their preparation for ministry. For the sake of those who have run aground in their journey, please share this book with them. They need to hear its message. Pray for them. Don't let them go (in the Spirit) until they have returned to follow the Lord in this Process. This is the work of the Spirit of God and we can cooperate with Him in His call to the Church to return to Him.

Prayer Partner

One of the greatest advantages we can gain in this Process is to find a partner in it. Our partner should be able to relate to where we are in the Process. We should pray for one another and use our gifts to minister to one another. Start by pursuing God in prayer for a partner, then thank Him for His answer and let Him lead you.

Location, Location, Location

I have sought the Lord many times to understand where I was in the Process. My motive was to get out of it, and fast. When I thought I knew where I was, it wasn't long before I discovered that I didn't. Most of my understanding of the Process has come in hindsight. I could not see forward but I could see the past with some degree of clarity. It is not as important where we are in the Process as it is to know we are in it. The Holy Spirit may not always follow this exact order. It is only an outline of what God wants to accomplish in our life. I have made many trips back to the Waters of Marah to deal with deeper levels of bitterness. The Process is three fold and death of the Flesh is required for our relationship with the Father, for our ministry to our family, and our public ministry. This systematic Process must not become the focus of our journey. It is only a guide for our warning, encouragement, and understanding. Our focus must be upon the love of our Father and our relationship of surrender to the Holy Spirit. Where we are is not as important as where we are going. Keep looking for and believing in the Promises which God has made to you personally, and to you as part of the Body of Christ.

This Process of sanctification is evident in both the theology of Scripture and in the lives of those who walked with God as described in the Bible. Walking through this Process will give us the opportunity to live portions of the lives of many of the people of the Bible. Things they said and did will prompt a "*been there, done that*" response which will confirm to us that we are on the same path they were on. Although God has given us a very clear example of His Process of sanctification in the story of the Children of Israel taking the Promised Land, there are many other characters of the Bible who confirm the stages and steps of His redeeming work.

Joseph's life was a prime example of the three stages of the Process. As a young boy, he was thrown into a pit, left for dead, and then sold into slavery (the Wilderness). He became prosperous in Potifer's house as the first indication of his ministry (entering the Promised Land). Just when He thought his life was looking up, Potifer's wife attempted to seduce Him (possibly a devoted thing). He passed the test and was advanced to the next stage of the Process (Seven Nations) when he was put in jail. He was released from prison through no effort of his own, and was made second-in-command of all the country. He was also given a signet ring as a symbol of authority. The equivalent of this for us, is the authority inherent in the resurrection of the Spirit Man.

There are many other examples in Scripture of this Process. Despite this abundant confirmation, there are times when doubt can still overwhelm us. The things the Spirit will lead us into are so unlike what we see with our natural eyes that it is not difficult to feel lost and confused. There are many people who have made this journey in the Wilderness but it is rare to meet one just at the time of doubting. The Spirit will not let us depend on anyone but Him. Occasionally God will do some very personal and intimate things to confirm His love and reassure us that we have not missed His leading. His affirmation is meant to open our eyes of faith again. His love revives us and touches us at the very core of our being. It is His love that gives us the assurance to go on in our Journey.

One of those events that assured me and touched my innermost being, was connected to a popular song which was written and performed by Billy Joel called "*River of Dreams*". When I heard the song for the first time, I cried because I knew that the song expressed for me my journey in the Wilderness. It expressed my doubts and fears, frustrations and longings. Each line of the song meant something special to me about my journey. The next four times I heard the song on the radio, I "lost it". I become concerned and inquired of the Lord why I was so emotional when I heard this song. He said, "*I have caused this man to prophesy to you*". The song was a "word" from God for my life. I knew God saw all my doubt and fear in the Process and loved me in spite of it. This experience became part of the deep healing and restoration He was doing in me. Months later, I asked the Lord if I was just dreaming in "Technicolor" or was that really Him? I was doubting again. "*Would He confirm that this song was really for me*"? A short time later I was at a large conference at which there were delegates from Australia. They called several of the leaders to the platform to give a word of greeting. One of the Pastors said, "*as silly as it may seem, the Lord has used a song by Billy Joel called "River of Dreams" to minister to me*". Later when I spoke to the man, he prophesied to me wonderful words of comfort and affirmation and the love of the Father. He will never know how much the Lord did for me at a difficult time through him. Even to this day when I hear the words of this song I am touched by the love of God. He can and will do *anything* to encourage us just when we need it

We put no stumbling block in anyone's path, so that our ministry will not be discredited. Rather, as servants of God we commend ourselves in every way: in great endurance; in troubles, hardships and distresses; in beatings, imprisonments and riots; in hard work, sleepless nights and hunger; in purity, understanding, patience and kindness; in the Holy Spirit and in sincere love; in truthful speech and in the power of God; with weapons of righteousness in the right hand and in the left; through glory and dishonor, bad report and good report; genuine, yet regarded as impostors; known, yet regarded as unknown; dying, and yet we live on; beaten, and yet not killed; sorrowful, yet always rejoicing; poor, yet making many rich; having nothing, and yet possessing everything.
2 Cor. 6:3-10 NIV

Chapter Ten

The Victorious Church

....and to present her to himself as a radiant church, without stain or wrinkle or any other blemish, but holy and blameless. Ephesians 5:27 NIV

The Coming Church

No one would argue that today's Church is not without stain or wrinkle. There are "hot spots" of power and authority throughout the world, but for the most part, the Church has been accurately called, "*The Sleeping Giant*". Preachers speculate that this could be the year that the Lord will return. Yet if He returns now, even by human standards, the Church is not ready. Something dramatic must happen to prepare us for Jesus' return. We must be purified and sanctified and set aside as wholly unto the Lord. We must be empowered with authority over death and every evil thing. We must wear the full armor of God and walk in the Spirit in every aspect of our spiritual life. We should regularly raise the dead and see heathens fall down before the Living God. We are headed for the greatest unfolding of power and authority the Church has ever seen. Greater things will be done in the last days than in the former days. This is where God is taking us. He is calling those who will, to be part of that victorious Church. In our humble circumstances, God is preparing us to rule and reign over every power on earth. He is preparing an army who will overcome spiritual forces much greater than ourselves. He is purifying His people in preparation for being released into a new authority. He is going to give us His signet ring so we can rule over all things in this Age and the Age to Come. Of course, we have to be broken and surrendered to Him before we are fully prepared for that ministry.

When Jesus walked the earth, there were only two people that we know of who were filled with the Holy Spirit: Jesus and John the Baptist. Jesus spent His time in the Wilderness, but John became known to LIVE in the Wilderness. He was a man who did not comply to the society of that time. He was a voice in the Wilderness crying out to the people to prepare the way of the Lord. John's words where prophetic but so was his life. He had physically separated himself from the world by the inspiration of the Holy Spirit. His life is a prophetic word to the Church of today. God will call many into the Wilderness to become outcasts of our society in order to call the Church into preparation and purity for the return of the Lord. These latter-day John the Baptists will not baptize in water but in fire. This cleansing fire will bring those who will, into obedience to the Holy Spirit. These "Forerunners" will be persecuted by portions of the Church and the world. They will be the fearless Gideon's army who will not love their life even unto death. There will be an army of prophets and apostles who like the disciples gave themselves up for the Body of Christ.

No Plan "B"

And the LORD thy God will bring thee into the land which thy fathers possessed, and thou shalt possess it; and he will do thee good, and multiply thee above thy fathers. And the LORD thy God will circumcise thine heart, and the heart of thy seed, to love the LORD thy God with all thine heart, and with all thy soul, that thou mayest live. Deut. 30:5-6

"The days are coming," declares the LORD, "when I will punish all who are circumcised only in the flesh— Egypt, Judah, Edom, Ammon, Moab and all who live in the desert in distant places. For all these nations are really uncircumcised, and even the whole house of Israel is uncircumcised in heart." Jeremiah 9:25-26 NIV

These two prophecies reveal that it was God's intention to transform Hearts **right from the beginning**. They reveal that the promise made to Israel was really being made to us. The promise was to purify our Hearts and set a people aside wholly for God. This could not have been possible except through the transformation and the forgiveness of Jesus and the sanctifying work of the Holy Spirit. God's leading of the Children of Israel in the Wilderness could therefore be for no other reason than what was stated in 1 Corinthians 9, which was to provide for us understanding and to give us a warning. God's purpose for leading the Children of Israel in the way He did was to demonstrate to us His plan of sanctification. It is clear in Scripture that God arranged the events of their journey. His purpose was to warn Believers in this last great latter rain of the Holy Spirit not to resist Him in His sanctifying process. God established a physical Promised Land primarily to reveal Himself and His plan of sanctification to us. He did not fail with Israel and then go to plan "B". He always intended to have a people of pure Hearts toward Him. Throughout history, He sanctified individuals but before Jesus returns, He will sanctify His Body so they will be adorned with wedding garments without spot or wrinkle. The promise to Abraham by God to redeem a people who would be the New Adam is fulfilled only through the forgiveness of Jesus and the sanctification of the Holy Spirit in the Wilderness.

The outpouring of the Holy Spirit and the increasing number of Believers in the Wilderness are signs of the time. They point to a season of purging for the Body of Christ and the return of Jesus very soon. All of what has happened from Adam's fall until now is pointing to us as the circumcised of Heart people of God - the Church today. He is making us the fulfilment of His promise to Abraham.

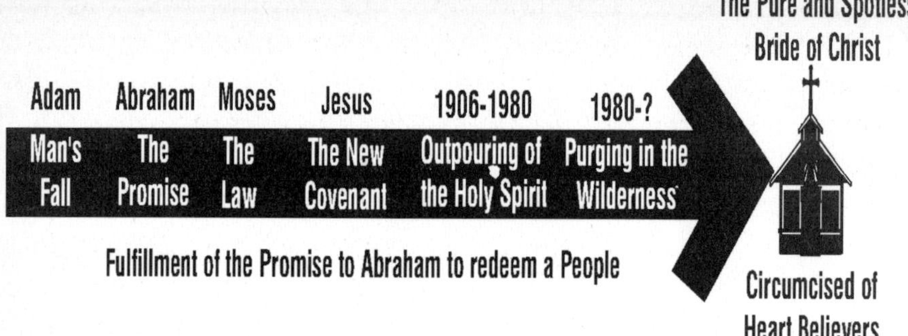

Valley Of Decision

God will escalate the pace and speed by which people will go through the Process. What took some Believers 15 or 20 years in the past may only take two or three years to accomplish in the future. Persecution and economic disorder will be two of the catalysts for our purging as a Body. This will reprioritize our values. Some of us will cling to God while others will go off into the world and its system looking for a temporal solution to their problems. We are not far from a "storm" of persecution and difficulty which will strip the Body of Christ of its vanity and materialism. That storm will drive every Believer into a valley of decision. We will either depend on the Holy Spirit entirely and allow Him to lead us through a barren land, or refuse Him. Jeremiah 9:25 says, God will punish the circumcised with the uncircumcised because they were uncircumcised of Heart. This journey is not optional. We will follow the Holy Spirit or we will be like the first generation of Israel, stubborn, and rebellious and unfruitful in the purpose God called them to.

And before him shall be gathered all nations: and he shall separate them one from another, as a shepherd divideth his sheep from the goats. And he shall set the sheep on his right hand, but the goats on the left. Then shall the King say unto them on his right hand, Come, ye blessed of my Father, inherit the kingdom prepared for you from the foundation of the world. Matt. 25:32-34

He cuts off every branch in me that bears no fruit, while every branch that does bear fruit he prunes so that it will be even more fruitful. You are already clean because of the word I have spoken to you. Remain in me, and I will remain in you. No branch can bear fruit by itself; it must remain in the vine. Neither can you bear fruit unless you remain in me. "I am the vine; you are the branches. If a man remains in me and I in him, he will bear much fruit; apart from me you can do nothing. If anyone does not remain in me, he is like a branch that is thrown away and withers; such branches are picked up, thrown into the fire and burned. If you remain in me and my words remain in you, ask whatever you wish, and it will be given you. This is to my Father's glory, that you bear much fruit. Matt. 15:2-8 NIV

Globalization

Globalization is a mania that is sweeping the world. It is being presented as inevitable and based upon *free* trade. When you examine it, however, there is nothing free about it. It is an attempt by a relative few companies to dominate and control the production of goods and services on a worldwide basis. An elite group of companies are positioning themselves through mergers and acquisitions and the use of international governing bodies to dominate the worldwide supply of a particular service or group of products. These companies are using domestic and international governments as tools of their purpose. Globalization is "economic communism". It is the spirit of control, domination, manipulation, and the centralization of power which is a manifestation of the nature of the Flesh. The Flesh is anti-Christ. The Spirit and the Flesh are at enmity with each other. They are the antithesis of each other, therefore the Flesh is anti-Christ. Where Jesus and the Holy Spirit are there is freedom. Where the spirit of Antichrist is there is control, manipulation, domination, tyranny, greed and the other manifestations of the Flesh. Control dominates and destroys freedom. Globalization promises freedom but whenever control is centralized in the hands of a few, it ends in tyranny. There is one yet to be revealed who will take over the domination of the world and he will do it with the assistance of the Devil through the power of the Flesh which is manipulation and domination and control. He will say "yes" to the Devil when tempted in the Wilderness with the kingdoms of the earth. He will be deceived by his Flesh. He will become the Antichrist.

The Flesh and the Devil must succeed in their domination of the world for then the stage will be set for Jesus' return. The day is coming that it will be impossible to buy or sell without the "mark of the beast". That is control. That is the spirit of Anti-Christ. We (the Body of Christ) were born subject to the Flesh, but would it be appropriate for Jesus' Church to be operating in the Flesh instead of the Spirit? Would any manifestation of the Flesh be appropriate in the Church as we approach the final confrontation between Christ and the spirit of Anti-Christ? How could a house divided against itself stand? It is necessary for Jesus to purify His Body completely of the Flesh, so it will be the pure and spotless Bride for whom He is returning.

The birth of the Age to Come will be preceded by a brief period of tribulation which is part of the process of bringing the old order ruled by the Flesh to an end, and the birth of the new order ruled by Jesus Christ. The Holy Spirit uses disorder to bring about His order. This is a picture of the process of sanctification. Even the world will go through this Process by way of the Great Tribulation. For those who have been through the Process, they will be fully prepared for this. They will be familiar with the Process and even find it exciting. What will be birthed will not be the Resurrected Man but the physical rule and reign of Jesus Christ on earth for a thousand years. Jesus is preparing His Body to rule with Him. We must be dead to the Flesh and having been tested in the Wilderness found to be faithful. In the midst of turmoil, God is at work humbling, testing, and bringing new life. The Flesh hates chaos because it is out of control. God will bring chaos in the Wilderness for Believers and the Great Tribulation for the world as preparation for the birth of the Lordship of Jesus Christ on earth. In spite of our failings as the Body of Christ, we will be ready for the return of Jesus. Those who love Jesus and who are looking for His return will not be disappointed. He will fully prepare those who will accept His invitation to the Wedding Feast. They will not show up in rags. They will be beautiful and radiant in purity and power.

"The kingdom of heaven is like a king who prepared a wedding banquet for his son. He sent his servants to those who had been invited to the banquet to tell them to come, but they refused to come. "Then he sent some more servants and said, 'Tell those who have been invited that I have prepared my dinner: My oxen and fattened cattle have been butchered, and everything is ready. Come to the wedding banquet.' "But they paid no attention and went off— one to his field, another to his business. The rest seized his servants, mistreated them and killed them. The king was enraged. He sent his army and destroyed those murderers and burned their city. "Then he said to his servants, 'The wedding banquet is ready, but those I invited did not deserve to come. Go to the street corners and invite to the banquet anyone you find.' So the servants went out into the streets and gathered all the people they could find, both good and bad, and the wedding hall was filled with guests. "But when the king came in to see the guests, he noticed a man there who was not wearing wedding clothes. 'Friend,' he asked, 'how did you get in here without wedding clothes?' The man was speechless. "Then the king told the attendants, 'Tie him hand and foot, and throw him outside, into the darkness, where there will be weeping and gnashing of teeth.' "For many are invited, but few are chosen." Matt. 22:2-14 NIV

Persecution

What can be shaken will be shaken, and as it shakes what is not built on Christ will collapse. The character, authority, and giftedness developed by the Holy Spirit in our lives will stand for all eternity. It will be part of our treasure in Heaven. Persecution must come for it is part of the process of purification and preparation. It will come from within and from outside the Church. There will be a division in the Church. Those that will enter the Wilderness and learn to walk in the Spirit will oppose those in the Church who are operating in the Flesh. They cannot exist together. Those in the Flesh in the Church will oppose those in the Spirit because they will not observe the Law. They will persecute those who are led by the Spirit. They will judge them to be in the Flesh. Those walking in the Spirit will be put out of the Church because they will be considered infidels, lawless, "crazies", and troublemakers. This is not unlike the things of which Jesus was accused. They will be despised by those operating in the Flesh and there will be a great division in the Church. Rick Joyner's prophetic word speaking of a coming civil war* may well be the battle in the Church between the Flesh and the Spirit. I see this division already appearing. Those walking in the Spirit will be outcasts and unqualified in the eyes of some people in the Church. They will judge in the pride of the Flesh with Scripture, not understanding however, that when we are controlled by the Holy Spirit we may appear to be misguided and foolish. If we believe the Holy Spirit is respectable and orderly, He is not. He is in the center of chaos, bringing redemption and Hearts of pure gold to adorn His temple. (* See the last page for more information)

The Flesh will not give up without a battle and the Anti-Christ will be the one through whom the Flesh and the Devil will battle against the warriors of God. They will use the power of the government to persecute the Saints of God. The Spirit led Church will not participate in the world's system and will be condemned and persecuted for it. This trap will be subtle and seemingly harmless but it will be a trap that only the Spirit of God can warn us of. Many will be lost at this time because they will not see with spiritual eyes what is happening. They may know prophecy and Scripture but like the Pharisees, they will miss Jesus. They will not be able to discern the true Body of Christ or walk in the Spirit. The Flesh will carry them away into deception, because it is an enemy greater and more powerful than them. It can only be defeated by the Holy Spirit. Many will choose the works of the Flesh without realizing what they are doing. Many will be lost, but many, and much will be gained.

The Devil and the Flesh will be defeated and Jesus will establish His rulership over the earth. His redeemed servants will be fully prepared to serve Him in that rulership. They will be proven and pure in motive and unable to be tempted by evil. It will be a wonderful time. Those who are experienced in battle will be well prepared for the things that are to come. They will understand how to defeat the Devil and the Flesh by the power of the Holy Spirit. There will be nothing to fear. It will be a glorious time of victory. It may seem like defeat in the natural eyes but then Jesus will return to justify all things. The "birth" of the Kingdom of God on earth will not come without turmoil. These minor trials will be an opportunity to overcome this world and to store up treasure in Heaven. The prophets of the Bible saw only vague visions of what was to come. We will be a part of it.

For I say unto you, Among those that are born of women there is not a greater prophet than John the Baptist: but he that is least in the kingdom of God is greater than he. Luke 7:28

The Army Of God

The Prophets Joshua and Caleb and all the valiant men of Israel took the Promised Land and subdued it. The women and children and all their possessions became benefactors of God's grace. There is a vanguard of valiant men and women being prepared to take the land by force. They will prepare the way as John the Baptist did for Jesus. They will be like the storm troopers of an army who will spearhead the attack. They are the FORERUNNERS of the Age to Come. They are a "Voice in the Wilderness" crying, "*prepare the way of the Lord, make straight His path*" (Matt. 3:3). They will work to bring reformation to the Body. They will lead and stand when the shaking and collapse of this world's systems brings millions of people to Christ for salvation. This shaking will also drive the Church into a final valley of decision. When our life is threatened and all the vanity of this world has failed, then Jesus and His promises will be all that we can hang on to.

Being obedient to the Holy Spirit will be of tremendous importance in this troubled time. If we turn to the right or to the left, it may mean the difference between life and death. It was that way for many of the first century Christians and it will be also for us who will usher in the New Age. All of this is just the beginning of the most wonderful time in the history of the Church and man. The Church will be glorious, undefeatable and demonstrating power and authority. The victorious Church will not be a visible Church that is ruling and powerful but an invisible Church. It will be like a 5th column in the midst of its enemies. It will be made up of the despised and outcast and those least likely to appear like rulers. Jesus' followers were the losers of their time. It will be difficult to see with natural eyes a victorious army but with Spiritual eyes, it will have authority over nations and over the Flesh and the Devil and the world. It would be a mistake to imagine a Church who is glorious in anything else but the Spirit. In the natural, it may well appear to be quite pathetic and foolish to those who cannot see it with spiritual eyes. Isn't that God's way?

For it is written: "I will destroy the wisdom of the wise; the intelligence of the intelligent I will frustrate." Where is the wise man? Where is the scholar? Where is the philosopher of this age? Has not God made foolish the wisdom of the world? 1 Cor. 1:19-20 NIV

A New Generation

In spite of their bondage, Israel had a love for the things of Egypt. At one point they longed for the leeks and onions of their former life. They had forgotten the cruelty of their slavery. They were deceived. They didn't want to go through all this hardship to get to the Promised Land. They wanted comfort and pleasure and as little struggle as possible. A generation of Israel died in the Wilderness because of their love of pleasure and unbelief. It was the next generation who was born in the Wilderness who became the "believing generation". They had not been ensnared by the bondages and pleasures of Egypt's system. Being born in the Wilderness, they had nowhere to go but forward. They understood it was God who had them there and they were willing to trust Him. In the last 40 years, God has baptized more people in His Holy Spirit than in any time in the history of the modern Church. Many of these people followed the Holy Spirit into the Wilderness. Some have completed the journey but most are stuck there. They have become entangled with the things of this world and have not been able to move forward because of unbelief. They are dying in the Wilderness. The Spirit of God is calling to this generation who are stuck in the desert to believe that He is the rewarder of those that seek, believe, and trust Him for the Promise. Many Believers have given up the pursuit of the Promise and have sought the comforts and pleasures of the world. They are building businesses and wealth which will perish with them. Where their treasure is, so also is their Heart. It is difficult for those who have been born into the slavery of the world's system to leave it. Some will return to the Lord (their first love) and follow Him, but many will not. It is the next generation who will become the "believing generation". The new generation has little hope in the systems of this world. They can see it is doomed to fail. They have not enjoyed the short term pleasures of this world. They can see the folly of man's works and the hope of the coming Kingdom of God. They have not tasted of the bondage of Egypt. They have no expectation of its survival. They are prepared to overthrow it and usher in the Kingdom of our Lord. They will be prepared to sell all to acquire the "pearl of great price". It will be the new generation who will become in a large part, the victorious Body of Christ. This does not exempt others from entering the promises. There was a remnant of Believers from the elder generation of Israel who trusted God. This prophetic teaching is a message of hope to **all** who will choose life and fruitfulness; and it is a warning to those who have become ensnared by the deceit of riches, the cares of this world, and the rebellion and deception of the Flesh.

Then he told them many things in parables, saying: "A farmer went out to sow his seed. As he was scattering the seed, some fell along the path, and the birds came and ate it up. Some fell on rocky places, where it did not have much soil. It sprang up quickly, because the soil was shallow. But when the sun came up, the plants were scorched, and they withered because they had no root. Other seed fell among thorns, which grew up and choked the plants. Still other seed fell on good soil, where it produced a crop -- a hundred, sixty or thirty times what was sown. He who has ears, let him hear." Matt. 13:3-9

A New Temple

The promise in Scripture that the Temple would be restored is often believed to be the physical Temple in Jerusalem. The Lord is rebuilding the Temple but it is not a temple of bricks and mortar. It is a temple filled with the gold and silver of the righteous deeds of the Saints. It is the circumcised of Heart who have been refined as pure gold, and who are fully prepared for the Master's use. WE are the temple of the Holy Spirit. Prophecy is for understanding of events as they happen, and to confirm the work of God after the event has happened. There were 800 prophecies about the Messiah which were well known by the Pharisees. They studied them and looked for His coming but they did not see Him when He came. They used carnal understanding to see things that can only be seen by the enlightenment of the Holy Spirit. The Pharisees were sincere and devoted believers in God, but carnal. They missed Jesus and His Kingdom when He came because they did not have spiritual eyes to see. They were not humble. Their knowledge caused them to judge things in their own understanding. If we use our own understanding to interpret prophetic Scripture, we will miss Jesus when He comes again, just like the Pharisees. We must not depend on anything other than the Holy Spirit and walk humbly with Him. In humility and surrender there is complete safety. The New Temple will be built of the only thing worthy to be in it - pure gold made by the Holy Spirit. There is nothing we can do of ourselves that would ever qualify to be part of the Temple. We can only surrender to the work of the Holy Spirit and let Him make us into something beautiful. If you are in a difficult time right now, you can rejoice because your humbling circumstances will produce pure gold in you to adorn the restored Temple of God.

Understanding and Warning

God has called those who will, to enter and continue in this Process. You may already be in the Process and the word of the Lord to you is, "victory is imminent". The reward of faithfulness is eternal. The time is short and the battle is not to the strong but to those who depend on God for victory.

Some readers have entered the Wilderness and have run aground on discouragement, bitterness, hardness of Heart, or have turned back from their destination. Some have become mired in coping habits or devoted things that prevent the Holy Spirit from leading them on to the next level. Whatever the circumstances or the condition of the

Heart, I pray that these words will reaffirm your vision for your destiny in God. I trust that it will be a map for you of the journey that will reveal God's ways of working His character and purposes out in His people. It is a warning to us that we should not resist the Holy Spirit when He is leading us into the death of the Flesh. Hopefully, it will call back to life some "dry bones" and visit a dying generation in the Wilderness with faith and a cup of cold spiritual water.

"A Journey in the Wilderness" is a book about walking in the Holy Spirit and not about dos and don'ts and principles. It is a book about the Spirit of God and His "ways" with His people. It is intimate and precious to God because these are the ways of a Bridegroom with His chosen Bride. He is preparing us for the Wedding Feast of the Lamb. He is preparing us to love Him fully and to live and reign with Him for all eternity.

But we have this treasure in jars of clay to show that this all-surpassing power is from God and not from us. We are hard pressed on every side, but not crushed; perplexed, but not in despair; persecuted, but not abandoned; struck down, but not destroyed. We always carry around in our body the death of Jesus, so that the life of Jesus may also be revealed in our body. For we who are alive are always being given over to death for Jesus' sake, so that his life may be revealed in our mortal body.
2 Corinthians 4:7-11, NIV

A Journey In The Wilderness
Information

The Forerunner: If you would like to join a community of people who are making their way through the Wilderness, you can find out more by visiting the Forerunner website at: **http://www.theforerunner.net** The site features a free E-Zine (electronic magazine) and opportunities to interact with others who are in the Wilderness. New areas are being added to the site as the demand for more interaction becomes evident, so drop by and visit and discover how you can contribute and connect with others.

Book Orders: Available through most bookstores. If you would like to locate a distributor please contact us by e-mail at: **info@theforerunner.net**

Comments: If you have comments about "*A Journey in the Wilderness*", you may e-mail them to, **comments@theforerunner.net**

Seminars: A Journey in the Wilderness is also available as a seminar to Churches and conference groups. More information about this and our other seminars can be had by contacting the author by E-mail, at: **seminars@theforerunner.net** or visit The Forerunner website at, **http://www.theforerunner.net**

Rick Joyner's prophecy entitled "*The Coming Civil War*" can be seen at: **http://www.morningstarministries.org** or by contacting, Morning Star Ministries, P.O. Box 19409, Charlotte, NC 28219-9409,

Distributed In Canada By
Rainbow House
1-800-265-8887